FRENCH *Drawings*

FROM PRUD'HON
TO DAUMIER

FRENCH

Drawings

FROM PRUD'HON TO DAUMIER

Introduction by Maurice Serullaz
Conservateur du Cabinet des Dessins au Musée du Louvre

 *New York Graphic Society*

GREENWICH, CONNECTICUT, U.S.A.

Library of Congress Catalogue Card Number 66-19493

© in France by Editions Art et Dessins S.A. 1966
Printed in Italy

Printed by Amilcare Pizzi S.p.A., Milan, Italy

THIS BOOK HAS BEEN
COMPILED AND EDITED
BY ANDRÉ VANTOURA
WITH THE ASSISTANCE
OF O. H. GASNIER

ACKNOWLEDGMENTS

This book has been made possible through the generous cooperation of the following museums and private collections:

Musée du Louvre, Paris
Musée des Arts Décoratifs, Paris
Ecole des Beaux-Arts, Paris
Musée Gustave Moreau, Paris
Musée du Petit Palais, Paris
Maison Victor Hugo, Paris
Musée des Beaux-Arts, Lille
Musée Condé, Chantilly
Musée Fabre, Montpellier
Musée Boymans, Rotterdam
The Metropolitan Museum of Art, New York
Collection of Dr. Oskar Reinhart, Winterthur
Collection of Dr. Peter Nathan, Zurich

The editors wish to express their special gratitude for the assistance of Miss Rosaline Bacou and Mr. Maurice Serullaz, Curators of the Cabinet des Dessins in the Louvre. The notes and biographies have been edited by Arlette Calvet (A.C.) and Geneviève Monnier (G.M.), assistants in the Cabinet des Dessins in the Louvre, and by Lise Dunoyer (L.D.).

This edition has been translated from the French by Florence Hammond Phillips, with the editorial assistance of Linda Boyer of the Print Department of the Metropolitan Museum of Art.

LIST OF ILLUSTRATIONS

David

Gérard

Girodet

Guérin

Ingres

Courbet

Millet

Daumier

INTRODUCTION

French drawing enjoys an altogether unique position of prestige in France itself, and since the days of Fouquet and the Clouets there has always been a pronounced taste for this medium among French artists. This can perhaps be attributed to a temperamental bent for analysis, which is equally manifest in French literature, and as the nineteenth century brought no diminution in this concern, drawing, during this period, showed itself to be more complex and richer in possibilities than ever before. From Prud'hon to Daumier, who stand at the two chronological poles of this study, all French painters without exception were draughtsmen, no matter in which of the great schools of painting they were classified: Neo-Classicism or Classicism, Romanticism or Realism.

"Feeling and drawing—these are the two true masters from whom one can learn to wield a brush," stated David, the leader of the Neo-Classic movement, to his friend Wicar in 1789, and in this sentence he seems to be handing us the key to the two divergent—indeed contradictory—trends which marked painters' attitudes toward drawing during this period. For one group, Neo-Classicists and Classicists, drawing was to be the essential base, the absolute foundation of any art, and occasionally, like Ingres, they were to carry the exclusive cult of line and arabesque to an obsessive pitch. In the opposite camp, Romanticists and Realists turned to drawing as a direct and spontaneous means of expression, finding it a medium for liberating their fever and their passion. The fact remains, however, that whatever may have been the spirit in which they approached drawing, all these French artists did reserve a choice place for it in their work.

The need for individualism, which had been extolled by the Revolution, and which the Romantic Era would push to the point of paroxysm, was now introduced into art, and because drawing allows the individual to express himself in a more directly personal way than painting does—providing a more faithful reflection of the most profoundly "true" personality of the artist— it was bound to be the area which took greater liberties with given models and established rules. This new freedom could already be felt even among the Classicists, despite their ties to tradition, and it proceeded to blossom and expand with the Romantics and the Realists. Drawing lost something of the original quality of a study or exercise, and acquired the characteristics of "handwriting" peculiar to each creator. It became, one could say, the means for a sort of "graphic journal," whereby daily reality could be relived through the medium of individuality. Subjects were no longer limited to religious scenes, mythology, allegory, history, to copies of the ancients or the old masters; instead they extended to all of life, to the point that Delacroix could say: "Everything is a subject." We make note, furthermore, of the fact that the subject of *Man* has always presented a powerful attraction for the French painters, in whom psychological observation is constantly a temptation. All the artists to be discussed here will hold to that path: but one must bear in mind that as far as *Man* is concerned, every artist is really always pursuing his own identity—his own self. Breaking with the often anecdotal intimacy of drawing of the preceding century, in the nineteenth century the medium took on a quality of avowal, of bearing witness; and here lies the interest for anyone who seeks understanding of the artists' contribution to the glory of French painting in an epoch when foreign schools provided only weak imitations or unoriginal vestiges of their past in opposition.

No study of the artists between Prud'hon and Daumier leads to the discovery of a uniform development in either drawing or painting. Whatever development there was found itself influenced from all sides; we see it hesitate, turn back on itself, set out on divergent paths; it is multiple, and does not permit of constricting definitions which are too general and too simplistic.

Prud'hon, an isolated individual difficult to place within the framework of any school, is the person who establishes the transition from the eighteenth to the nineteenth centuries. His frontier position is not without an analogy to that of Jean-Jacques Rousseau, whose *The New Eloisa* (*La Nouvelle Héloïse*) was, in fact, illustrated by Prud'hon. Rousseau, the author of the *Confessions* and the *Reveries of a Solitary* (*Rêveries d'un promeneur solitaire*), introduced

Romantic ferment into literature right at the peak of eighteenth-century rationalism—and what turmoil that was to produce in the future! Prud'hon, who fully preserved the poetic charm and refined grace of the past century, emerges on the other hand as the precursor of such divergent tendencies as Neo-Classicism and Romanticism—both of which were to reach their full flowering in the century which then was just beginning.

Prud'hon's interest in antiquity and the paintings of Herculaneum and of Pompeii is obvious, but the feverish melancholy in his work looks ahead to the agitation of the Romantic era. There is something reminiscent of the Mannerist style, of a Correggio, of a Parmigianino, of a Pietro da Cortona, in the elongation of his female bodies, in the expression of dreamy ecstasy in his faces; but he often substitutes virility for the sensual languor which he would have inherited from the eighteenth century, as for instance the decorative panels for the *hôtel de Lannoy*, whose plastic beauty even Degas could not deny.

Prud'hon's technique is equally complex. He generally make use of natural black chalk or stumped charcoal (estompe), with large white highlighted areas on grey or blue-grey paper. Incisive accents of light are imposed on the deep velvety blacks, in order to suggest the contrasting effects of chiaroscuro: "It is the drawing of light which he seeks above all else," said the Goncourts. But the stump also permits him to obtain a sort of gradation of forms which gives a softened, vaporous quality to his drawing. Finally, sometimes he defines his modelling in space by a seemingly disorganized network of crosshatched lines.

The Romantic state of mind underlying Prud'hon's work does not find any echo either in Boilly, who specialized in the portrait and in genre scenes giving a faithful reflection of Revolutionary and Imperial customs, or in Isabey, who was the official portraitist of the Empire, and later of the Congress of Vienna, and whose miniatures are as precious as any documents for giving us a knowledge of the noteworthy personages of his time.

With David, the reformer, it is quite another current which comes into play. Reacting against whatever there was of the facile, the light, the libertine, in eighteenth-century art, he ordained a return to the grand manner, the heroic subjects inspired by antiquity; and an entire school of painting grew out of the laws he laid down. For a long time David has passed for a correct but cold draughtsman. Certainly the copies of antiquities which he executed during his youthful sojourns in Rome offer only a rather meagre aesthetic interest. But from that same period come some rare and extremely sensitive landscapes, wherein he lingers over subtleties in the play of light and also reveals himself in flagrant contradiction to the theories of the Neo-Classic school, of which he was the uncontested head.

In most of his drawings an aspect of his personality appears which is often absent from his paintings. He reveals himself as being more human, more natural than one would imagine from his rigorously doctrinaire pronouncements; and although he harked back to the memory of Poussin and Le Brun, he is proof of that individualism mentioned previously. Without seeking to make any rules in this area for his pupils, David the draughtsman often managed to combine the stylistic grandeur and nobility of thought of his predecessors with a sense which could already be called realistic, and with a touch of melancholy and unrest which is not untinged by Romanticism.

While the pen and wash studies for his compositions inspired by antiquity did remain subject to academic constraint, those done in pencil, black chalk, or pen, for subjects drawn from contemporary history such as the *Sacre*, show a surprising freedom of energy. The line bursts out and flashes with incomparable spirit. As a portraitist David does not always escape the conventions of posing, but his psychological gifts, his objective qualities (pushed often to the point of cruelty, as in the famous sketch of Marie-Antoinette on her way to the scaffold), unfailingly lead him to create a real and vivid image of his subject.

Portraiture has always been a fertile area of French genius in any age; it also appealed to a disciple of David, Gérard, who devoted himself to it almost exclusively after the failure of his canvas, *Psyche Receives the First Kiss from Cupid* (*Psyche reçoit le premier baiser de l'Amour*), at the salon of 1798. Though he remains faithful to the Neo-Classicism of his master, his style is tinged with a mannerist quality which is not without a certain preciosity and is particularly noticeable in his pencil sketches for portraits, or in his charcoal studies for decorative works. On the other hand, his genre sketches done in pencil heightened with wash are quite akin in their greater freedom of execution to the works of one of his English contemporaries, Constable.

Dependence upon antique models and a search for purity of contour were the essential principles for another pupil of David, Girodet, but the contagion of Romanticism did induce him to look for new sources of inspiration. Thus we find him illustrating an episode from Chateaubriand's *Atala*. But while this choice of a contemporary literary subject, this attraction for exoticism, and this taste for Nature, all indicate separation from the strict Neo-Classical doctrine, Girodet's rendering itself still conforms to it. The studies for *Atala at the Tomb* (*Atala au Tombeau*) done in natural chalk or in charcoal highlighted with white, even more perhaps than the finished painting, reveal the fundamental disaccord between Girodet's elegiac sentimentality and the passionate vigor, the eternally inexhaustible imagination, the stylistic color and warmth, of that would-be painter story-teller, Chateaubriand. We will have to wait for Delacroix and the *Natchez* before encountering any pictorial interpretation worthy of the author of *The Genius of Christianity* (*Le Génie du Christianisme*). Although some of Girodet's compositions such as *The Judgement of Midas* (*Le jugement de Midas*) seem to prepare the way for the symbolism of a William Blake, or even to look ahead to certain aspects of surrealism, the chilly conventions of academism are found in his studies for *Phaedra* (*Phèdre*), which only retain the most artificial side of the theatre, allowing nothing of the trembling passion of Racine's drama to be felt.

The same is true of Guérin, who was the pupil of a rival of David, Jean-Baptiste Regnault, and who in the preliminary studies for his paintings tries vainly to master the tragic expression. His plastic conception bears some relationship to that in drawings by the Neo-Classic sculptors, Chaudet, for example.

But it was not until Jean-Auguste-Dominique Ingres, whose whole work was a tireless quest for the stylization of form, that the linear style reached its apogee. Though he came out of the Neo-Classicism of David, this artist discarded it; David and his emulators Gérard, Girodet and Guérin, drew inspiration from sculpture in high relief or Roman bas-reliefs, but Ingres preferred the arabesque to volume, and looked to the Greek vase or to Raphael as his sources. In his case, contrary to the principles of Neo-Classicism, it was not a question of "copying" forms according to the models provided by Roman antiquity and according to a canon of proportions which had been defined once for all without any room for personal interpretation. Ingres redesigned the human body in accordance with his own ideals by a series of "distortions" (which led Odilon Redon to say, "but Ingres is the one who makes monsters"), and in so doing he revived the graphic purity of Greek vases, infusing it with the spirit of the Florentine mannerists and the School of Parma.

Ingres, who was certainly classical, but who was an outstanding innovator of forms, can be placed at the root of certain directions in modern art, the art of Modigliani or of Matisse, for example. In his studies of female nudes, the line of the composition is supple, voluptuous, sinuous, all curves; the light areas are indicated by fine lines, while he makes use of more heavily applied lines to suggest the volume.

While he is an extraordinary subjective portraitist, Ingres chooses a different style when he wishes to establish the general image of his contemporaries in individual or collective portraits: *The Stamaty Family* (*La Famille Stamaty*), *The Forestier Family* (*La Famille Forestier*). There he frankly separates himself from the conventions of the antique and from the Italian masters, and portrays his models with the most objective exactitude, by placing them in their own milieu, that of the conformist bourgeoisie of his time. In scrutinizing with the greatest sharpness the exact detail which, according to him, will define "the" character, he comes close to the analytical spirit of the Flemish and Dutch masters.

Ingres the draughtsman often eclipses Ingres the painter. Empassioned by the refined play of line which he developed into the complexity of the arabesque, he possessed a science of drawing permitting, as he said "the profound study which great purity of form exacts."

As we have already mentioned, the fever which enlivened the Romantics, their cult of the self, their exaltation of individuality were all even better expressed in drawing than in painting. Pen, wash with contrasting shadows and light, water color, all became favorite media for those painters who were pursuing life in all its forms. They gave less importance to pencil because its precision was better suited to the detailed work of Ingres than to their own impetuous ardor.

We find intimations of Romanticism beginning in the very entourage of David himself, as a reaction against his intolerant dogmatism. Gros, the pupil to whom David had to entrust the continuation of his atelier when he was exiled, was torn between his own Romantic aspirations and his loyalty to his master's imperative theories; and he found suicide the only way out of the conflict bought on by being the pivotal figure between two such opposed forms of expression.

"In anguished transition from the immobility of David to the tumult of Delacroix," as Elie Faure has excellently put it, Gros turned to the dramatic contrasts between life and death proscribed by the David aesthetic. His workmanship is very free, his technique rapid, effortless. This freedom comes out above all in his pen drawings, which are of a violence that no longer owes anything to Neo-Classicism.

One of the great milestones of the Romantic movement, the first performance of *Hernani* in 1830, finds an echo in a little-known but interesting painter, Granet. This artist from Aix, a pupil of David, gave his chief attention to the problem of light. Using contrasts of chiaroscuro in religious scenes lit by torches, or luminous, vibrating color effects and variations of atmosphere in landscape water colors which already seem pre-Impressionist, his work marks an important step in the evolution of landscape painting. And Victor Hugo himself, the uncontested leader of literary Romanticism ("*The Preface to Cromwell*," Théophile Gautier writes, "shines like the tablets of the Law on Mount Sinai") was beguiled by the possibilities of plastic expression. In numerous drawings and water colors he tried to surpass the value of words, and to fix in some way other than verbal imagery the phantasmagorial visions of his inexhaustible imagination.

Romantic painting also needed a leader when it was in full swing, and only Géricault's premature death in 1824, the very year in which *The Massacres at Scio (Les Massacres de Scio)* was painted, kept him from having this role which was assumed instead by Delacroix. Like Delacroix, Géricault's Romantic ardor was tempered by a search for balance; his own powerful temperament led him to instill passion and life into his classic training, and to conquer the mastery of form. In his vigorous, virile art he used deep contrasts of lights and shadows, modelling his bodies in masses, in the sculptural manner of Michelangelo. Drawing holds a preponderant position in his work, and he was concerned with a variety of techniques: pen washed with sepia for the copies from antiquity which he did at the outset of his career; water color for the "portraits" of horses whose plastic beauty he caught better than anyone else; black chalk for the studies preparatory to his *Wild Horses Racing* (*Course de chevaux libres*) and, for the mythological compositions in chiaroscuro on tinted paper, wide flat areas of white gouache spread out to indicate the planes of light. But it was the pen which best suited the violence of Géricault's temperament, permitting him a nervous, vibrant, seemingly confused graphic style which is actually carefully constructed and organized according to his governing idea. His short but fiery career provides the necessary bridge for connecting Rubens to Delacroix.

"Can one conceive that the spirit does not guide the artist's hand?" wrote Eugène Delacroix, thereby delivering to us one of the keys to his own work, wherein the idea always plays a decisive part and a lucid intelligence controls his feverish imagination. This is particularly evident in his innumerable drawings: Delacroix is probably the most prolific draughtsman of the nineteenth century. Everything, for him, provided a pretext for drawing, and he was one of the artists who was most successful in keeping the sort of "graphic journal" which we mentioned earlier. One thinks specifically of his Moroccan sketchbooks, but all his studies, spread out over the years, permit one to trace the genesis of his paintings and decorative works, and to understand better his deepest intentions. The fertile inventiveness, bold research and accomplishments, and the impetuous touch of this imaginative artist all combined to reinvent form. He himself stated: "Nature is a dictionary;" he dipped into it certainly, but he then recreated it to suit himself. His drawing, less sculptural than that of Géricault, is essentially a painter's drawing, and all the techniques are present: pencil as well as Conté crayon, pen as well as charcoal, wash as well as water color and pastel. One can see a clear evolution from the extremely correct sketches done while he was very young, under the influence of his master, the Neo-Classicist Guérin, to the studies for his large decorative works, in which the live dynamic quality of his line makes the form spring into relief, even though the classical balance is never abandoned.

From 1822 on, his style established itself, became freer, more passionate, more tumultuous, and in his dramatic intensity he did not always shrink from using exaggerated means of expression. In 1825 a voyage to England introduced him to the water colorists Fielding, Bonington, and Constable, providing an experience which enlarged his ability for evoking atmosphere in landscapes.

His studies executed between 1826 and 1831 for *Sardanopolis*, the scenes from *Faust*, or *Liberty Leading the People* (*La Liberté guidant le peuple*) give trembling suggestions of movement arising out of whirlwinds of lines, ovoids, and networks of arabesques. These are "forms in action." Then his voyage to Morocco in 1832 revealed to him the live beauty of antiquity and invested his impetuously romantic vision with a nobility and grandeur which are altogether classical. Meanwhile his discovery of light led to a pre-Impressionist use of vibrant touches of color done with quick juxtaposed brushstrokes. By this time, and right on up to the end of his career, Delacroix possessed full mastery of his art: the mastery of recreating form in all its meaning, the mastery of unfailingly expressive color, and the mastery of totally integrated thought. He is related to the great Venetians, to Raphael, to Rubens. But far from being simply turned toward the past, he stands as the *avant-garde* of the whole of modern art, from Impressionism to our own day. One man did recognize how much painters who came after Delacroix owed to him, and this man himself is one of the greatest. It was Cézanne, who said: "All of us are painting in him!"

Something of Delacroix's stylistic power and the same attraction he felt for the savage nobility of wild beasts, can also be found in the animal sculptor and painter, Barye, who was as fine a draughtsman as he was a sculptor. He employed a very individual technique in his water colors. Because he considered water color by itself too fluid, by mixing it with Indian ink and gouache highlights, he obtained a granular appearance, a dense texture like that of oil painting. He observed live animals in the Jardin des Plantes, or in a zoo in Saint-Cloud, and in an effort to evoke Africa or Asia he set them in imaginary landscapes painted from sketches done in the forest of Fontainebleau.

Still another sculptor, Carpeaux, also has a place in the history of French drawing. His numerous and very free sketches, in charcoal or in black chalk, recapture Parisian life at the time of Napoleon III, and all the pomp of the receptions at Compiègne. His direct observation of nature also comes out in his portraits and in his *Dancers* (*Danseuses*) who opened up for him the multiple possibilities of movement through variations in a plastic medium.

The work of a pupil of Gros, Charlet, who was the official historian of the Napoleonic campaigns and the chronicler of military life at the time of the Empire, never rises above the level of anecdote. Géricault, however, accorded him the title of the "La Fontaine of painting" and Delacroix addressed such eulogies to him that one is rather taken aback: "In looking over the series of magnificient drawings which mark chiefly his first mature period, one finds oneself involuntarily wondering what, in the work of the greater masters, could be preferable to his rendering of simplicity, conception, and scale in drawing." In our day and age the talent of Charlet seems far more modest.

An instantaneousness of vision and a discernment of the essential set Constantin Guys beyond the narrow limits of anecdote, while he pursued with an attentive and curious eye the image of a brilliant and frivolous society. "A painter of modern life, he is a genius," wrote Baudelaire, "for whom no aspect of life is uninteresting. He seeks that something-or-other which we may be permitted to call modernity. It is he who will sift out of fashion whatever she may contain of poetry in the midst of history—he will extract the eternal from the transitory." Guys' innumerable drawings are almost always executed by following an indentical process. After a rapid sketch in chalk, heightened with water color or wash, he points up his contours with chalk to define the planes of shadow.

It was Chasseriau's wager to undertake a synthesis between the two divergent magnetic poles which had French painting on the rack: i.e. the linear obsession of Ingres on one hand, and Delacroix's passion for color on the other. He was a disciple of Ingres, as he reveals above all in his pencil portraits, where his pure line attempts precise definition of both the character and the strict physical likeness of his models. But a certain exotic languor (Chasseriau was born in Santo Domingo) pervades the faces of his women, and this duality led Théophile Gautier to say: "He is an Indian who studied in Greece." Equally classical are the studies he did for vast decorative works: the churches of Saint-Merri, Saint-Roch, Saint-Philippe du Roule, and the stairway of the Cour des Comptes, which was partially destroyed by fire during the Comune.

From the many sketches and water colors which he brought back from a journey in Algeria, we see that he was a great admirer of Delacroix; but this orientalism is tainted by the picturesque, and never arrives at that sense of the permanent which Delacroix achieved. Finally, Chasseriau was also an extremely cultivated man and often displayed a marked taste for symbols, thereby paving the way for the pronounced symbolism of his pupil, Gustave Moreau. Opposing himself to his contemporaries, the Impressionists, who were bringing to life on canvas the world which they saw before their eyes, Gustave Moreau engendered a fantastic universe, peopled with strange creatures, wherein allegory played an essential role. Even if he analyzed nature before departing from it, it was only in order to penetrate the world of magic and dream more successfully, and to attain: "that abstract *Beyond* which transports the spirit and the soul into the rare and sacred domains of imagination."

Certain obsessive themes recur in his work: Salome, Helen, Pasiphae, Dalila, Medea whose stories he treats tirelessly over and over again, in a sort of pitiless reproach against womankind. The position he adopted in relation to art was never anything but literary, and there again he separated himself from the Impressionists, who entrusted themselves totally to their instincts. For Gustave Moreau "art must elevate, ennoble, moralize." And what were the means to achieve this? Substitution for the reality of phenomena something which he himself called "androgynous nature," the "necessary richness," and the mystical visions—verging on abstractions—of his own "interior sentiment." These symbolist meanings are translated into highly charged compositions, where his emblems pile up in a rather excessive luxury of detail, but it is in his water colors, which are surprisingly modern in their technique, that one sees the best of Moreau's graphic work. Here he is making discoveries about the tonality of colors, whose power he deeply recognized: "One must think about color, one must have imagination about it. If you have no imagination, you will never make a beautiful color. Color must be thought, dreamed, imagined."

Moreau's influence on certain artists of the twentieth century who were his pupils is perfectly evident. Despite their totally different personalities, Matisse owes to Moreau his graphic purity, his stylization of form, his love of the arabesque, while Rouault assimilated his mystical expressionism, though he brought to it a new dimension from the spirit of the Middle Ages.

With the momentum of the Romantic movement, which advocated a return to nature—as much in literature as in art—landscape assumed a prime position in painting and drawing during the nineteenth century, and several stylistic currents began to run side by side. One of the greatest landscapists of all times, Camille Corot, aligned himself with the Classic tradition, keeping unbroken ties with artists like Claude Gellée or Poussin. All through the years drawing was one of his constant preoccupations: "To draw every evening," he says in his notebooks, or, again: "to my mind two things of prime importance are the rigorous study of both drawing and tonal values." His work as a painter was nourished by the same acute sensitivity as his work as a draughtsman. Whether we examine the pencil or pen studies from the first half of his career, or the drawings in stumped charcoal, which was his preferred medium at the end of his life, we will always find, combined with his concern for harmoniously ordered rhythms and his need for realism, a penetrating sense of subtle values, an intelligence in the line, and a comprehension of whatever subject he chose to represent, all of which are far from frequent in the history of art.

At the time of his first sojourn in Italy, from 1825 to 1828, Corot was drawing in very hard pencil cut to a fine point, or in pen, views of the Roman countryside, of Civita Castellana, Ariccia, Nemi, Frascati, Marino; and there is a precision in the details of these drawings, a scrupulous consciousness of form and a very pure graphic sense, which make them worthy of the Primitives. In the following years, however, he tempered this rigorous structure and care for minutiae to make way for a sensitive and subtle search into the nature of tonal values, and this concern persisted, no matter whether he was working in Italy, where he returned in 1834 and 1843, or in the French provinces.

The year 1848 was a milestone in the evolution of his style. His vision renewed, he no longer sought anything except poetic evocation of a scene—all built up through infinitesimal tones—and he limited his landscapes to their general masses and planes, in order to create the atmosphere specific to a place. From 1860 on, obsessed by the problem of light reflection and the fleetingness of visual impressions, Corot inclined toward reverie and melancholy, and his art belongs to both the real world and a fairy universe. He drew on tinted chamois paper, brown or grey, and without giving up the pencil and pen he often used charcoal to obtain deep velvety blacks; the stump permitted him certain "submerged" vaporous effects. Then with a few highlights in white chalk he would mark the glittering of light and its diffused reflections through mirages of mist. His landscapes, wherein nature is always civilized, are animated by phantom silhouettes of nymphs and heroes which seem to be apparitions rather than real beings.

But we must not limit Corot's art purely to that of a landscapist. All his life he loved and studied the human figure, whether painted or drawn. In pencil portraits and studies of nudes he went beyond the simple reality of his model and made it "poetic," through the dreamy expression of a look, or a pose stripped of all conventionality. His characters are not posed; they are "sketched," seemingly right in the midst of the excitement and the truth of a direct conversation with the painter.

Another trend in landscape painting of this time harked back to Holland in the seventeenth century, to Ruysdael or Hobbema. Following their example, it was to the pathetic, tormented force of nature (which was well in agreement with the vehemence of Romantic feeling) that certain painters gave their attention. Théodore Rousseau was the leader of this group, which called itself the Barbizon School; and he managed to reconcile Romanticism with Realism through concepts which were opposed to the more humanistic ones of Corot. To subtleties of atmosphere, Rousseau preferred contrasts of light, violent sunsets rather than morning mists. In his drawings, generally done in pen, the structure of trees and the planes of the earth are defined in rapid, vigorous strokes, and he completely conveys the sense of space. Sometimes, also, his more detailed, more copious technique links him to the landscapes drawn by Breughel the Elder.

Among the other members of the Barbizon group, Daubigny often used chalk or pen to evoke the ephemeral aspects of nature, such as reflections on water; while Harpignies chose water color heightened by gouache, a medium which permitted him to portray the sundrenched Mediterranean landscape as successfully as the finer nuances of the Ile de France or of Morvan.

These landscape painters were certainly realists, but the term "Realist School" is used to designate the movement which arose at the time of the Revolution of 1848, as an offshoot of Romanticism. More or less marked by the socialist and humanitarian theories of thinkers like Proudhon, the artists of this group interested themselves in contemporary political and social events, and gave an almost proselytizing quality to their works which attempted to express the misery of the common people.

Rustic life and work in the fields found an incomparable bard in Millet, whose art achieved a solemn and moving poetic quality. His drawings very often eclipse his paintings, and, with Ingres, Delacroix, Daumier and Degas, he stands as one of the greatest draughtsmen of the nineteenth century. Though his concept of subject matter was traditional, his handling of plastic elements shows astonishing diversity, and indicates that he did not retreat from the new spirit of audacity of his time. Pissaro, Seurat and Van Gogh were all to learn from him. Pissaro was inspired by Millet's sketches of peasants, in black chalk, wherein networks of lines release the fullness of his forms; Seurat used, in his own graphic work, the intense velvety blacks and many variations in half-tones of Millet's charcoal and black chalk drawings; while in Van Gogh's work we find the dramatic, even hallucinatory tension, and stiff brushstroke technique which Millet had used in certain studies, such as one of his masterpiece, the famous *November*.

His numerous sketches of peasants, harvesters, and reapers show a profound, innate sense of gesture which is both simple and noble and which is always compellingly true to life. His stripped-down, de-emphasized contours, his large, full, often synthetic line, express only what is essential, the eternal truth. His landscapes, rather than being faithful images of places, are hymns to a bountiful Mother Earth and to her cyclical rhythm. Calendars and seasons come alive through his drawings with even more realistic intensity than they do in the miniatures of medieval Books of Hours. The spontaneity of his "impressions" in drawing prepare the way for the canvas impressions of someone like Claude Monet and the visual revolution of Impressionism, which would soon completely upset the traditional axioms of painting.

The man in whom the spirit of the Revolution of 1848 and the aesthetic of the Realist school are best incarnated, actually drew very little. Gustave Courbet was in fact a painter first and foremost, and instead of the severity demanded by line, he preferred the richness and fullness of a generous impasto, applied almost brutally with a palette knife; and this technique is certainly more strictly in keeping with the vehement, revenging spirit of this ardent defender of the working classes. His drawings in pencil, pen, and above all, black chalk and charcoal, do not always have the plastic force of his canvasses, nor the same sturdiness of conception or freedom of execution. Some of his portrait drawings, however, are remarkable for their directness of accent.

But to take quite an opposite case, Daumier was an artist who owed the better part of his work to drawing. This incomparable interpreter of human passions gave rise to an inexhaustible repertory of form which he was constantly renewing and in which he was the equal of Ingres and of Delacroix. He was a realist, but he almost never worked directly from nature; he drew from memory on paper or on lithographic stone absolutely faithful images—the fruits of his tireless observation. All techniques were familiar to Daumier: pencil, which created motion and volume through a network of very fine lines; Indian ink wash, which in vigorous accents of shadows and lights defined planes and intensified his volumes; pen, which pointed up the essential quality of his model in rapid touches while he then went over it in pencil to reinforce the shadows, giving a sculptural quality to his masses; and water color, used for large highlights in flat tones.

After 1848 the taste for grandeur and monumentality, combined with the Baroque tendencies derived from Michelangelo and Puget, gave way to the investigation of light and its vibration—an investigation which established itself as the forerunner of Impressionism, as it was to be re-formulated by Cézanne. Themes borrowed from everyday life, and sometimes treated with Goyaesque violence, became more and more frequent, and the satirical verve of the artist who stigmatized the weaknesses and vices of society was now given free rein, without ever falling into the easy lap of anecdote.

His pen may have been cruelly sarcastic in portraying *The Judges (Juges), The Doctors (Médecins), The Lawyers (Avocats),* but Daumier always leaned toward the common people with greater understanding, attentive to human misery, whether physical or moral. A few incisive lines were enough to underline a grimace, capture an agonized moment, or freeze the forced grins of his *Saltimbanques*; and when he took his inspiration from literature he looked to the great satirists as his sources: Molière, La Fontaine, Cervantes. But his preference ran, incontestably, to the "modernity" preached by Baudelaire—modernity which he found in the street, in shops, and in the railway trains immortalized in *The Third Class Carriage (Le Wagon de troisième classe).*

As we have said above, the art of drawing, from Prud'hon to Daumier, is essentially multiform, but while the great currents which run side by side are certainly often divergent, both in their conception and in their realization, it also often happens that they overlap, and it is possible to try to follow some evolution, to unravel some unity. Artists began to reject the constraints of past centuries, and this freedom led them in turn toward change in the very subjects of their art. Deserting the fiction of a "beau ideal," they moved progressively toward direct observation of nature and of reality as they experienced it. "Modernity" invaded their work, and they took upon themselves this statement by Baudelaire: "Woe to him who studies, in antiquity, anything other than pure art, logic, and general method. If he delves too deeply he loses his memory of the present; he abdicates the value and the privileges furnished him by circumstance. For almost all our originality comes from the stamp which the climate of the time imprints upon our sensations."

Maurice Serullaz

FRENCH *Drawings*

FROM PRUD'HON
TO DAUMIER

Pierre-Paul PRUD'HON Cluny 1758 - Paris 1823

Prud'hon was born April 4, 1758, the last child in a numerous family, and was raised by the monks of Cluny until he was put in the charge of the painter Antoine Devosges, of Dijon. He came to Paris in 1780, worked in the studios of Wille and Pierre, and in 1784 obtained the *Prix de Rome*. In Italy he enthusiastically discovered the painters of the Renaissance: Leonardo, Raphael, and above all Correggio, whose art was to influence him all his life. On returning to France in 1789 he encountered difficulties, but being party to the Revolution he received several commissions from the revolutionary government and was able to survive by painting portraits. The Directory and the Consulate were periods in which his reputation grew; the prefect of the Department of Seine-Frochot commissioned him to do large decorative works, notably one for the Hôtel de Lannoy which brought him to the attention of Napoleon and Josephine. He became their most favored painter, and, in her turn, Marie-Louise engaged him as her drawing master. This was the most successful period of Prud'hon's life. His various submissions to the Salon received triumphant acclaim: *Innocence Prefers Love to Riches* (*L'Innocence préfère l'Amour à la Richesse*), *Divine Vengeance Pursuing Crime* (*La Vengeance divine poursuivant le crime*), *The Abduction of Psyche* (*L'Enlèvement de Psyché*) — Louvre — but unfortunately his success did not continue. After the fall of the Empire, he had difficulty resuming work and undertook large paintings, such as a *Crucifixion* for the Cathedral in Metz, without being able to finish them. The suicide of his pupil and friend Constance Mayer in 1821 contributed to the sadness of the end of his life; he died February 16, 1823.

Being simultaneously an historical painter, a portrait painter, a painter of decorative works, an illustrator, and a designer both of monuments and of *objets d'art*, Prud'hon is an artist who establishes the transition between the eighteenth and the nineteenth centuries. He was a fervent admirer of antique form, but his classicism was interpreted through an entirely Correggesque sensuality, and the subtle modelling in his drawing, his chiaroscuro effects, and the emotion inherent in his work, made him also the harbinger of Romanticism.

A.C.

1 Innocence Surprised by Love

(L'Innocence surprise par l'Amour)

Black chalk, heightened with chalk, on blue paper
13 by 16⅛ in. (33 by 41 cm.)

Chantilly, Musée Condé

"A breath, a cloud, a sketch, which is easily the most poetic and most passionate depiction of amorous desire." The judgement of the Goncourts justly defines the character of this drawing, which belonged to the Duke of Aumale and is one in which Prud'hon has expressed youth and passion with an infinite degree of charm and intensity.

A.C.

Pierre-Paul PRUD'HON

2 Love's First Kiss

(Le premier baiser de l'Amour)

Pen and ink, black wash, heightened with white, on grey-blue paper
4¼ by 3⅛ in. (11 by 8 cm.)

Louvre — No. RF 1455

"In a grove, Julie, supported by Claire, receives Saint-Pieux's first kiss, as she places her arms about his neck in a swoon." One of five vignettes engraved by Copia for *Julie ou la Nouvelle Héloïse*, by J.J. Rousseau (new edition, Paris, 1804), this drawing is one of Prud'hon's most enchanting creations.

A.C.

Pierre-Paul PRUD'HON

3 Self-Portrait

Pen and brown ink
6⅛ by 4½ in. (15.5 by 11.5 cm.)

Louvre — No. RF 1580

Executed during his journey to Italy (1785-1789) this
"witty and elegant sketch" (Goncourt) whose workmanship leads one to believe that Prud'hon meant to
engrave it himself, had been sent to Dagoumer, a doctor
and friend of the painter. It was later engraved by
Jules Boilly with the inscription: "Prud'hon se ipsum
delineavit calamo - Jul. Boilly sc. Ex coll. P. Dromont."
                                                      A.C.

Pierre-Paul PRUD'HON

4 Study of a Nude Female Figure
(Etude de jeune femme nue)

Black chalk, estompe, heightened with white chalk,
on light blue paper
20⅛ by 13⅜ in. (51 by 34 cm.)

Paris, Musée des Arts Décoratifs - No. 16423

A study based on the model for the figure of the seated
Venus in the painting *Innocence, or Venus Bathing*
(*l'Innocence ou Vénus au bain*) executed in 1812 and
now in the Louvre. The admirable modelling of the
body, haloed in light, reveals to what extent Prud'hon
succeeded in reconciling antique purity of line with the
sensuality of Correggio.

A.C.

Pierre-Paul PRUD'HON

5 **Peace, or the Triumph of Bonaparte**
(La Paix ou le Triomphe de Bonaparte)

Pen and ink, brown wash
3½ by 6⅛ in. (9 by 15.5 cm.)

Louvre — No. RF 4633

This allegory, inspired by antiquity, is the first study
for the large painting of the same subject in the Chantilly Museum. The theme was suggested to Prud'hon
by Brun-Neergard: "(...you should know why he
did this drawing for me. Desiring to develop certain
ideas on peace, I took up my pen. I was no little sur-
prised, in reading over what I had just written, to see
that I had composed a drawing. The following day
I went to Prud'hon to discuss my project... Bonaparte,
the First Consul of the Republic, is sitting on a triumphal
chariot: Victory and Peace are at his sides. The Muses
accompany him in celebration of his glory, and following
him are the Arts, who are indebted to him for his an-
nexation of the masterpieces of Italy. Ahead of him
Games, Laughter and the Pleasures are dancing, surrounding one of their brothers who is carrying the long-
desired olive branch (...)".

A.C.

Pierre-Paul PRUD'HON

6　**Study of a Nude Male Figure**

(Académie d'homme)

Black and white chalk on grey paper
17½ by 9⅞ in. (45 by 25 cm.)

Paris, Musée des Arts Décoratifs — No. 16424

In its strong and subtle chalk modelling, this beautiful
drawing is a characteristic example of the numerous
life studies done by Prud'hon in his later years.

A.C.

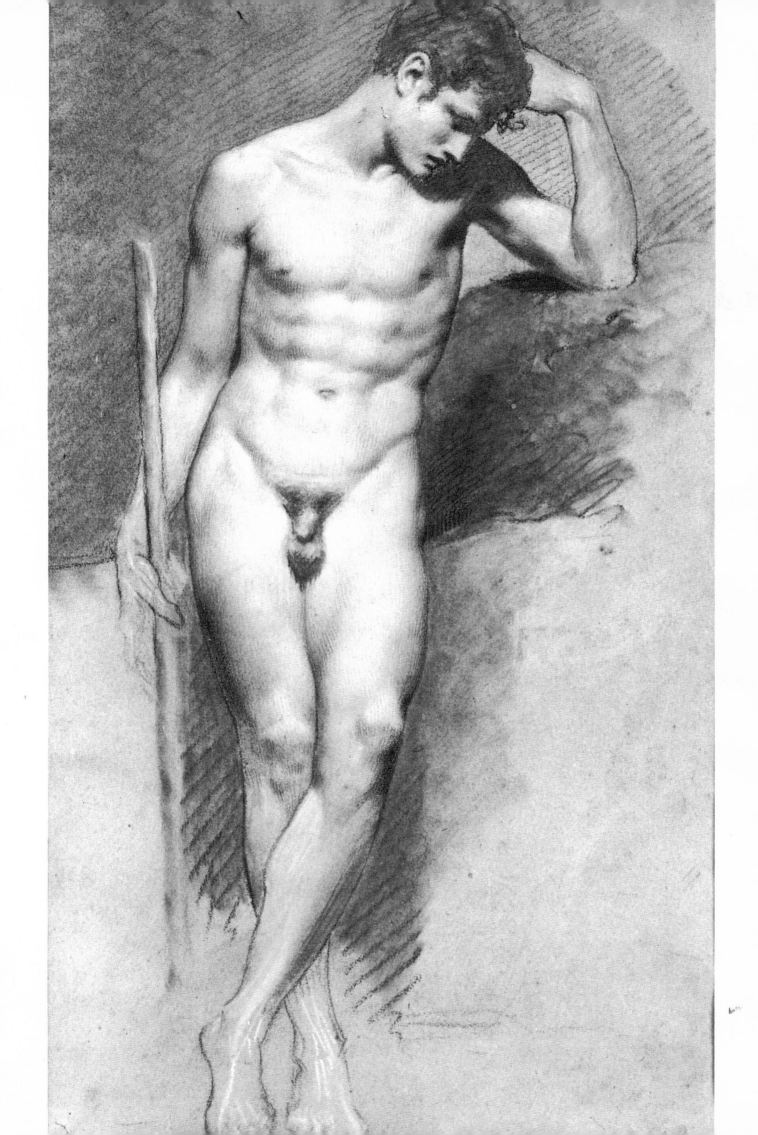

Pierre-Paul PRUD'HON

7 **Love and Friendship**

(L'Amour et l'Amitié)

(Black chalk, heightened with white chalk, on grey paper)
16¾ by 12⅜ in. (42.5 by 31.5 cm.)

Chantilly, Musée Condé

A study for the painting commissioned by the publisher Didot, and shown in the salon of 1793, though it remained unfinished. "The true genius of Prud'hon," writes Delacroix, "his domain, his empire, is allegory . . . the vaporous quality, this sort of twilight in which he envelopes his figures, strikes at one's imagination and takes it effortlessly into a world which is entirely the invention of the painter."

A.C.

Pierre-Paul PRUD'HON

A.C.

8 **Portrait of Monsieur Vallet
a Tax Collector**

(Portrait de Monsieur Vallet, receveur particulier
des Finances)

Brush and brown wash, heightened with white
6⅛ by 5⅛ in. (15.5 by 13 cm.)
Signed on the mount at lower right: P P P

Louvre — No. 1700

A study based on the painting exhibited in the Salon
of 1812 and now in the Louvre.

A.C.

Pierre-Paul PRUD'HON

9 Clotho, She Who Spins
(Clotho, la fileuse) circa 1804

Black chalk, heightened with chalk, on blue paper
12⅝ by 17¼ in. (32 by 44 cm.)

Chantilly, Musée Condé

One of three figures conceived as the decoration for the
pediment of the Hotel Dieu (1804). Guiffrey, Prud'hon's
biographer, reports that the project of representing the
Three Fates on the pediment of a hospital did not seem
a very good idea. The artist therefore modified his design
by adding to these figures a group representing Charity,
Hygie, and Aesculapius receiving a sick woman. In
any case the pediment was not adopted. The Musée
Condé also owns a study for the Second Fate: *Lachesis,
She Who Cards* (*Lachésis la Dévideuse*).

Louis Léopold BOILLY La Bassée (Nord) 1761 - Paris 1845

Having left home to paint first in Douai, then in Arras, where he executed a number of portraits, Boilly arrived in Paris in 1785. There he worked in the manner of Terborch or Gérard Dou, but went on to specialize in libertine subjects under the influence of Lavreince. Accused, during the Terror, of corrupting morals, Boilly justified himself by painting *Marat Carried in Triumph* (*Marat porté en triomphe*), Musée de Lille, and several picturesque scenes such as the *Standard Bearer* (*Porte-Drapeau*) or *The Civic Holiday* (*la Fête Civique*), Musée Carnavalet. But it was not until *The Arrival of the Stage-Coach* (*L'Arrivée de la Diligence*), 1803, Louvre, that he discovered his true style, showing in this painting the gifts of observation which made him so faithful and witty a chronicler of his time. Some years later the invention of lithography led him to undertake the famous series of *Grimaces:* physiognomical studies in comical and pleasing groups.

Boilly was a tireless artist who worked straight through to the last day of his life (January 6, 1845) without a sign of weakness. The considerable body of work which he left brings to life, both in intimate and in heroic poses, the actors in the tumultuous period during which he lived.

A.C.

10 Portraits of the Sculptor Martin and his Wife

(Portraits du sculpteur Martin et de sa femme)

Black chalk, heightened with white, on brown paper
7⅛ by 5½ in. (18 by 14 cm.)

Paris, Musée des Arts Décoratifs - No. 22-140, A and B.

As a portraitist, Boilly was extraordinarily productive, and the five thousand and more portraits which he painted of his contemporaries were greatly appreciated during his life because of "their polish and their likeness." These qualities are clearly apparent in this double portrait, which is treated simply and with great naturalness.

A.C.

Louis Léopold BOILLY

11   A Crossroads in Paris at the Time
      of the Revolution
      (Un carrefour à Paris à l'époque des déménagements)

      Chalk and water color
      18¾ by 26⅛ in. (47.5 by 66.5 cm.)

      Lille, Musée des Beaux-Arts

      First study for the painting exhibited in the Salon of
      1822. A small painted reduction of the same painting
      is now in the Musée Cognacq-Jay. This witty drawing
      illustrates Boilly's talent for depicting contemporary
      customs and manners.
                                                    A.C.

Jean-Baptiste ISABEY Nancy 1767 - Paris 1855

Jean-Baptiste Isabey came originally from Lorraine, but at an early age he left Nancy, where he had worked with Girardet and Claudet, to come to Paris and complete his training under the direction of the miniaturist Dumont and of David. After some initial difficulties, the patronage of Josephine and Bonaparte opened the doors of Malmaison to him and drew him closely into that circle.

Isabey was First Painter and Draughtsman of His Majesty's Cabinet under the Empire, and the organizer of public celebrations as well as private festivities at the Tuileries and Saint-Cloud; he rapidly acquired a wide reputation in the fields of portrait and miniature. The arrival of a new empress caused no change in the life of Josephine's protégé, for Marie-Louise made him her drawing master, and after the fall of the Empire, instead of sinking into disgrace, Isabey in 1814 was commissioned to paint the portraits of the plenipotentiaries at the Congress of Vienna. His brilliant career ended under Napoleon III, whom he served as Honorary Director of the Imperial Palaces. A remarkable draughtsman, and certainly the most brilliant miniaturist of his time, Isabey worked in both lithography and pastel, showing in these two techniques the same qualities of finesse and charm which characterize his water colors.

A.C.

12 Portrait of a Woman

(Portrait de femme)

Water color over black chalk
Oval. 14⅝ by 11¾ in. (37.3 by 29.9 cm.)
Signed at lower right in chalk: *Isabey*

Louvre - No. RF 4517

This ravishing portrait is characteristic of the freedom and subtlety which Isabey acquired in the treatment of water color. Working with light, transparent touches the artist has imbued the fine face of this unknown woman with an infinite seductiveness.

A.C.

Jean-Baptiste ISABEY

13 Return of Monseigneur
    the Dauphin's Expedition
    to the Ancient Chateau
    of Meudon, in 1791
    (Retour de la promenade de Monseigneur le Dauphin
    au vieux château de Meudon en 1791)

    Brush and grey wash heightened with white
    6 by 11 in. (15.2 by 27.9 cm.)
    Signed and dated at lower right in white: *Isabey, 1791*

    Louvre - No. RF 3820

    This is one of the only drawings which exists from the
    time when Isabey frequented the court of Marie Antoin-
    ette, though he made several miniatures in that period.
    In 1791 the artist married Laurice de Salienne who bore
    several children, one of them being Alexandrine, who
    is next to her father in the celebrated painting by Gé-
    rard in the Louvre. Another child was the painter
    Eugène Isabey.

                                                    A.C.

Jean-Baptiste ISABEY

14 Portrait of Napoleon

Brush and brown wash, over chalk
Oval. 5½ by 3¾ in. (13.2 by 9.6 cm.)
Signed and dated at left, in lead pencil: *Isabey 1811*

Louvre - No. RF 3836

Between the troubled period of the Consulate and the
glory of the Empire, Isabey drew Napoleon many times.
In 1811, a year after the Emperor's second marriage, to
Marie-Louise, the King of Rome was born and the
Louvre possesses a water-color portrait of him by Isabey,
painted fifteen days after the child's birth.

A.C.

Jean-Baptiste ISABEY

15 Portrait of Cherubini

Water color
4¾ by 3⅝ in. (12 by 9.3 cm.)
Signed at lower right in chalk: *J. Isabey*

Louvre - No. RF 3839

Luigi Cherubini was born in Florence in 1760, but established himself permanently in Paris from 1788 until his death in 1842. He composed several operas: *Lodoiska, Médée, Les Abencérages...*, and was named music director, then choirmaster, to the king in 1816 before becoming director of the conservatory in 1822. From this time on he devoted himself almost exclusively to religious music, composing a great many motets and cantatas as well as his admirable *Consecration Mass* which was played at the time of the installation of Ingres' *The Oath of Louis XIII* (*Vœu de Louis XIII*) in the Cathedral at Montauban. He also was the author of a *Treatise on Counterpoint and Fugue*.

A.C.

Jacques-Louis DAVID Paris 1748 - Brussels 1825

David's work and life are intimately tied to the history of his times in that they represent both an expression of and a triumph over the period in which he lived. Born at the height of the eighteenth century, David exhibited a passion for drawing even in his childhood, and though his tutors had not envisaged making a painter of him, they ended by taking him to Boucher, who later sent him to study with Vien. Once admitted to the course at the Royal Academy of Painting, the young man had to wait several years before obtaining the coveted *Prix de Rome.* In fact, not until 1774 was the prize awarded him with no opposition. A year later David left for Rome in the company of Vien, who was the new Director of the French Academy. He stayed there five years, drawing tirelessly from the great masters and the ancients. When he returned to Paris he became, in 1783, a member of the Academy. Upon receiving a commission from M. d'Angiviller for a painting, David chose *The Oath of the Horatii (Serment des Horaces)* as his subject, and left for Rome again in order to immerse himself once more in the atmosphere of antiquity. This canvas, in which he affirmed the primacy of line and stasis over color and movement and heralded a return to classic humanism, was sent to the Salon in 1785 and was acclaimed as the manifesto of the new school. But with the coming of the Revolution, David was pulled from history into reality. Passionate and militant by nature, he put his person and his art at the service of his country: he was a deputy at the Convention, a member of the *Comité de Sûreté Générale,* the chief organizer of revolutionary festivities and ceremonies. When he took up his brushes it was to illustrate certain tragic or heroic episodes of the time: *The Death of Marat (Marat assassiné)* 1793, Brussels, *The Oath of the Tennis Court (Serment du Jeu de Paume).* David's portraits reveal that he was a great observer of the whole human scene, as well as an admirable painter. After the fall of Robespierre he was twice imprisoned in the Palais du Luxembourg, and while in prison conceived his painting of *The Sabines,* Louvre, which he finished in 1799; but when he met Bonaparte and fell so strongly under that influence he once again abandoned the fanciful subjects of antiquity. He became Napoleon's First Official Painter, documenting the ceremonies of the new regime in such paintings as *The Consecration (le Sacre)* 1805-08, Louvre, and *The Distribution of the Eagles (Distribution des Aigles),* 1810, Versailles. Little by little his manner became cold and we see it reach systematization in *Leonidas at Thermopylae (Léonidas aux Thermopyles),* 1814, Louvre. At the time of the Restoration he exiled himself to Belgium where, surrounded by respect and adulation, he died in 1825.

David's greatness as a historical painter and as a remarkable portraitist gives him a fundamental position in the evolution of painting during the nineteenth century. The currents and developments which succeeded him could not be explained without taking into account the depth and significance of his art, and the reactions which it provoked.

A.C.

16 Two Studies of Heads
(Deux études de têtes)

Pen
6⅝ by 5⅜ in. (16.9 by 13.8 cm.)
Signed at lower right in pen and ink: *David fecit*

Paris, Ecole des Beaux-Arts - No. 737 and 739

E.B.A I2227

David fecit

E.B.A I2227

David fe

Jacques-Louis DAVID

17 The Oath of the Tennis Court

(Le Serment du Jeu de Paume)

Pen and ink, brown wash
25⅜ by 41⅜ in. (65 by 105 cm.)
Signed and dated at lower right: *J.L. David faciebat anno 1791.*
The figure of Bailly and the group including the Abbé Grégoire, Rabaut Saint-Etienne, and Dom Gerle were cut out and pasted on later.

Louvre. (Deposited at the Musée de Versailles)
No. RF 1914

Study for a painting commissioned in 1790 by the Jacobin Club and the Constituent Assembly to commemorate this important initial episode in the history of the French Revolution. David's execution of the grandiose work must have been interrupted by the turn of events at the time, for it was never finished. Among the numerous preparatory drawings which exist, this one, exhibited in the Salon of 1791 as No. 132, is characteristic of the artist's efforts to obtain a heroic composition. The theme of an Oath, which David had already attempted in the *Horaces*, Louvre, 1785, finds full expression here. "*The Tennis Court,*" wrote André Chénier in the *Journal de Paris* of March 20 and 24, 1792, "is one of the most beautiful compositions to which modern art has given birth, for it depicts a multitude of figures animated by the same sentiment, and concurring in the same action without being monotonous."

A.C.

Jacques-Louis DAVID

18 **The Sabines**

(Les Sabines)

Black chalk, pen, grey wash, heightened with white
18¾ by 25 in. (47.6 by 63.6 cm.)
Squared in chalk. Three strips of paper irregularly cut,
then pasted together.

Louvre - No. 26.183

This large drawing which belonged to M. Ingres is a
direct study for the painting which David had conceived
in September, 1794, while imprisoned in the Palais du
Luxembourg, and which he worked on five years later
(Louvre). Strenuously executed, but ample in its conception, it marks the artist's evolution toward a pure art;
the figures are posed with majestic immobility, indicating
David's desire to copy ancient Greek statues by increas-
ing the impersonality of this style. "My intention," he
might have declared as he painted this, "was to paint
the ancient customs with such exactitude that if the
Greeks and the Romans could have seen my work
they would not have found me a stranger to their ways."

A.C.

François-Pascal Simon GERARD (Baron) Rome 1770 - Paris 1837

Gérard was the son of an official in the service of Cardinal de Bernis, French Ambassador to the Holy See. He was enrolled in the Pension du Roi, founded by M. de Marigny; subsequently he entered the studios of the sculptor Pajou and of Brénet. Beginning in 1786 he was a pupil of David, and presented himself in the competition for the *Prix de Rome* which was given to Girodet. The next year he tried his luck once again, but work on his painting, *Daniel Vouchsafes the Chastity of Susanna* (*Daniel justifiant la chaste Suzanne*) was interrupted by the death of his father. He left for Rome with his mother, who was Italian, but had to hurry back to Paris where David took care of him and obtained lodging for him in the Louvre. Gérard was made a member of the Revolutionary Tribunal but did his utmost to avoid those terrible functions. It was in order to thank J.B. Isabey that he painted the portrait of that already celebrated miniaturist and his daughter in 1795 (Louvre). Despite the relative success brought, that same year, by his *Belisarius*, and by his *Psyche* (Louvre) in 1798, Gérard had difficulty selling his works and lived essentially from the drawings for Virgil and Racine which were published by the Didot brothers. It was not until 1800 that he became established as a portrait painter. The Emperor commissioned him to execute the official portraits, and in 1806 ordered from him a painting of *The Battle of Austerlitz* which Gérard did not finish until 1810. He was presented to Louis XVIII by Talleyrand, and was named Painter to the King after his *Entry of Henry IV into Paris* (*L'Entrée d'Henri IV à Paris*), Louvre, was exhibited in the 1817 Salon. At this time he also received the title of Baron. His career proceeded brilliantly under Charles X for whom he painted his *Sacre* in 1820, and under Louis-Philippe who commissioned from him the four pendentives which decorate the Pantheon (1832-36). He died at the age of sixty-seven after having produced more than twenty-eight historical paintings and three hundred portraits, all of which constitute a precious body of documentary work.

A.C.

19   Bust Portrait of a Young Woman

(Jeune femme vue en buste)

Black chalk, estompe, heightened with white
Circular. Diameter: 5¼ in. (13.5 cm.)

Louvre - No. 26716

In the simple treatment and controlled liveliness of this charming portrait we recognize Gérard as the direct successor to David.

François-Pascal Simon GERARD (Baron)

20   Head of a Young Woman

(Tête de jeune femme)

Black chalk and lead pencil, estompe, on beige paper
Circular. Diameter: 6½ in. (16.5 cm.)

Louvre - No. 26.717

Gérard excelled above all in his female portraits. The somewhat languorous and sensual aspect of this drawing, as well as its fine and sensitive graphic technique, make it a characteristic example of the artist's style as it was manifested in his portraits of *Countess Regnaud de Saint Jean d'Angely,* 1798, Louvre, or of *Marchesa Visconti,* 1810, Louvre.

A.C.

Anne-Louis GIRODET de Roucy-Triesen Montargis 1767 - Paris 1824

Girodet was left an orphan at an early age, was adopted by his tutor, the military surgeon Trioson, and after having learned the principles of drawing from the painter Luquin, entered David's studio in 1785 where he became one of the master's favorite pupils. He obtained the *Prix de Rome* in 1789 with *Joseph Recognized by his Brothers* (*Joseph reconnu par ses frères*), Ecole des Beaux-Arts, and left for Italy where he stayed five years. The painting he submitted to the Salon of 1793, *Endymion's Sleep* (*Le Sommeil d'Endymion*), Louvre, met with a great success, though its melancholy grace and lunar atmosphere came as a surprise. In 1801 the Emperor commissioned a canvas from Girodet for Malmaison. The subject of this painting was taken from Ossian's poetry, revealing the literary and romantic inclinations of the artist, who some years later was to undertake the interpretation of Chateaubriand in his most popular composition: *Atala at the Tomb* (*Atala au tombeau*), 1808, Louvre. Around 1810 his health took a turn for the worse, and he had no public showings until the Salon of 1819, where his *Pygmalion and Galatea* was exhibited. From this time on Girodet specialized in portraits.

Though he produced few paintings, he drew a great deal, and it is this aspect of his work which now appears as the most interesting, because of the purity of his graphic sense and the grace and lightness of his lines. This extremely cultivated artist was classic in form and was a believer in the pure contour, but his imagination was romantic, and he was open to new ideas. It is the duality of his talent which makes him appealing and reflects the evolution of taste at the beginning of the nineteenth century.

A.C.

21 Sheet of Studies

(Feuilles d'études)

Black chalk
10⅜ by 14½ in. (26.5 by 36.8 cm.)

Louvre - No. 26.780

Here Girodet gave final form to his studies for the death of Phèdre, clearly destined for the illustrations of *Racine*, published by the Didot brothers. The precise and linear graphic quality of this drawing makes it the herald of certain of Ingres' creations.

A.C.

Anne-Louis GIRODET de Roucy-Trioson

22 Atala at the Tomb

(Atala au tombeau)

Black chalk, heightened with white, on grey-brown paper
9¾ by 15¾ in. (24.9 by 40.1 cm.)

Louvre - No. RF 3973

This beautiful drawing is a study for the painting exhibited in the Salon of 1808 and now in the Louvre. It reveals a concern for line inherited from David, but in its indication of light it recalls the attraction which Correggio's painting held for Girodet.

Innumerable painters have been inspired by Chateaubriand's celebrated novel, but Girodet was actually personally intimate with the writer, whose portrait he painted in 1807, Saint-Malo Museum, and in this composition he faithfully presented the death of Atala in a pictorial medium. The Louvre possesses another study for the painting executed in the same technique (No. RF 3974).

A.C.

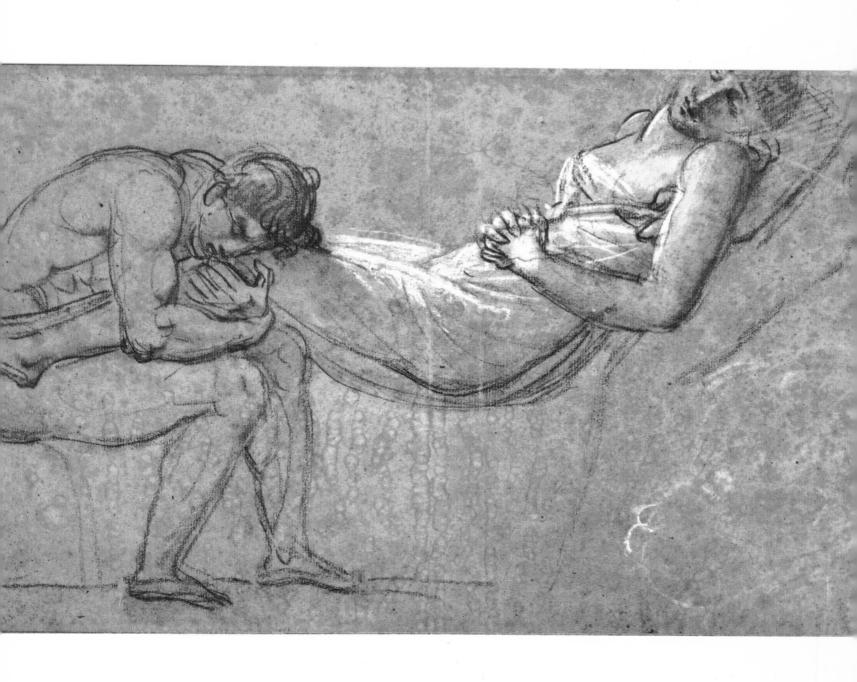

Pierre-Narcisse GUERIN Paris 1774 - Rome 1833

Nothing particularly attracted Guérin to painting until, on his father's advice, he finally entered first the studio of Brénet, then that of Régnault. After the great competitions were interrupted by revolutionary upheaval, there was instituted, in 1797, one single competition for the three prizes and Guérin was awarded one of them. Although no financial backing for the Rome fellowship had been re-established, the young artist nonetheless undertook all the work demanded of fellowship winners: by the time of the Salon of 1799 he had produced *The Return of Marcus Sextus* (*Retour de Marcus Sextus*), Louvre, which was crowned with extraordinary success not unmixed with political feeling, since the painting was treated as an allusion to the return of the émigrés. Once the French Academy had re-opened, Guérin left for Italy, spending time both in Rome and in Naples. When he returned, he continued painting from historical inspiration, but he also looked for subjects in poetry and drama, both of which passionately interested him, such as *Phèdre Accusing Hippolyte Before Theseus* (*Phèdre accusant Hippolyte devant Thésée*), 1802, Louvre. In 1816 he turned down the directorship of Villa Medici in order to stay in Paris, but he did accept the post when it was offered to him again in 1822. Guérin's bad health unhappily kept him from painting during his stay in Rome, but once he had come back to Paris in 1829 he wished to see Rome again, so despite serious illness he set off once more, accompanied by his successor Horace Vernet. He died several months after his arrival on July 16, 1833, and was buried at the side of Claude Gellée in the Trinità dei Monti Church.

A.C.

23 Sheet of Studies

(Feuille d'études)

Black chalk, pen, brown wash, heightened with white, (central section)
10⅜ by 16⅝ in. (26.9 by 42.1 cm.)
On the verso, a study of a draped male figure in black chalk; squared in black chalk.

Louvre - No. MI 595

The young boy at the right is a first study for the figure of Hippolyte in Guérin's painting, *Phèdre and Hippolyte* which was exhibited in the Salon of 1802 and is now in the Louvre. His rather declamatory pose shows how very often Guérin preferred theatrical artifice and exaggerated expression to the reality found in ancient painting and sculpture.

A.C.

Pierre-Narcisse GUERIN

24 Episode from Daphnis and Chloe
(Episode de Daphnis et Chloé)

Chalk, pen and black ink, brown wash
10⅛ by 12⅛ in. (25.8 by 30.7 cm.)

Louvre - No. 27031

In a clearing Philetas, sitting on a stone to the right, speaks to Daphnis and Chloe, who are seated in front of him near an altar laden with flowers and fruits. *Daphnis and Chloe* is a tale which originated among the ancient Greeks and was published by Longus in the fourth century A.D. It recounts the often thwarted love story of these two adolescents, found by shepherds, and it was adapted in French by Amyot and P.L. Courier at the outset of the nineteenth century. Innumerable artists have found subjects in it for their own inspiration.

A.C.

Jean-Auguste Dominique INGRES Montauban 1780 - Paris 1867

Born August 29, 1780, in Montauban, Ingres inherited his artistic vocation and his taste for music from his father, who was a cultivated ornament maker. At an early age he studied with Jean-Pierre Vigan, Joseph Roques and Jean Briant in Toulouse, and in 1776 he entered the studio of David. Five years later he won the *Prix de Rome*, but being unable to go to Italy immediately, he proceeded to undertake his portraits of the *Rivière Family* (Louvre) and *The Beautiful Zelia* (*La Belle Zélie*), Rouen. During his stay at Villa Medici (1806-10) and later in the course of the fourteen years which he was to spend in Italy, Ingres accomplished his best work in all fields. Working ardently, even though his situation in life was often precarious, he painted *Oedipus and the Sphinx*, Louvre, in 1808, sketched out several large projects such as *Stratonice, or the Illness of Antiochus* (*Stratonice ou la maladie d'Antiochus*), Chantilly, Montpellier, and finished among others the portraits of *Mme. Devauçay*, Chantilly, and *Granet*, Aix en Provence. In Florence, where he lived after 1820, he conceived *The Apotheosis of Homer* (*L'Apothéose d'Homère*), Salon of 1827, Louvre, but worked primarily on the painting commissioned by M. de Blacas for the Montauban Cathedral: *The Oath of Louis XIII* (*Le Vœu de Louis XIII*). When he was recalled to Paris by his success in the Salon of 1824, Ingres found that his reputation was established at last, and he opened a studio. But his position as head of a school and the heat of his artistic convictions aroused enmity which, when his *Martyrdom of Saint-Symphorien*, Autun Cathedral, was presented at the Salon of 1835, burst out with such violence that he chose to leave again for Italy. He was made Director of the French Academy and stayed in Rome from 1835 to 1841, when he returned to Paris as an uncontested master and did not stop working until his death. He undertook the decoration of the Château de Dampierre, executed numerous portraits, and at the age of almost eighty conceived the *Source* in 1856 and *The Turkish Bath* (*le Bain Turc*), Louvre, in 1859. He died January 14, leaving the greater part of his collections to his native city. The sovereignty which Ingres accorded to drawing above all other areas of expression provides the necessary unity in his immense and complex body of work. Maintaining a subtle accord between scrupulously observed reality and the exigencies of a style which imposed highly conscious distortions, Ingres, with his sensitive arabesque, conferred breathing vitality on his portraits and his nudes.

A.C.

25 The Forestier Family
(La Famille Forestier)

Lead pencil
9¼ by 12½ in. (23.4 by 31.9 cm.)
Signed and dated in lead pencil: *Ingres fecit 1806*

Louvre - No. RF 1450

Before leaving for the Villa Medici, Ingres was engaged to Julie Forestier, daughter of a judge and herself a painter and musician, but several years later Ingres broke off the engagement from Rome. In this lively and intimate portrait the artist has shown Julie Forestier in the company of her father, her mother, her mother's brother M. Salle, and the servant, Clotilde, thanks to whom the fiancés had been able to exchange a clandestine correspondence. The Musée de Montauban owns a replica of this drawing, also by Ingres.

A.C.

Jean-Auguste Dominique INGRES

26   Sheet of Studies
(Feuille d'études)

Lead pencil
6⅞ by 13½ in. (17.5 by 34.5 cm.)
Signed at lower left in lead pencil: *Ingres d.*
Inscription at upper right: *Mencuccia, via della vita 58*

Paris, Musée du Petit-Palais
Duthuit Collection: No. 1157

"In order to arrive at beauty of form, one must not proceed by square or angular modelling; one must model in the round, and without obvious internal details," said Ingres. This page of studies provides a definitive example of Ingres' love for line and contour, and is directly related to the *Odalisque and Slave* (*Odalisque à l'esclave*), The Fogg Art Museum, Cambridge, Massachusetts, which he painted during his second trip to Rome for Marcotte, a friend of his and the Director of the Ecole des Beaux-Arts.

A.C.

Jean-Auguste Dominique INGRES

27 Portrait of Madame Destouches

Lead pencil
15½ by 11 in. (39.5 by 28 cm.)
Signed and dated at lower right in lead pencil: *Ingres delineavit Roma 1816*

Louvre — No. RF 1747

The lead pencil portraits such as this one, which is drawn with almost ethereal delicacy, were always Ingres' most popular works and permitted him to subsist in Rome when the fall of the Empire momentarily deprived him of more important commissions. Armande Destouches, née Charton, was the wife of Louis-Nicolas Marie Destouches, an architect, the pupil of Vaudoyer and Percier, and winner of the *Prix de Rome* in 1814. The couple had just arrived at the Villa Medici when Ingres drew this fine portrait, without doubt one of his purest masterpieces.

A.C.

Jean-Auguste Dominique INGRES

28 Stratonice, or the Illness of Antiochus

(Stratonice ou la maladie d'Antiochus)

Lead pencil, traces of brown wash
11¼ by 15¾ in. (28.7 by 40 cm.)

Louvre - No. RF 1440

Ingres attached great importance to this subject which
was strongly in vogue at the end of the eighteenth century and had been treated by David, among others.
Ingres painted it twice: in 1840, Chantilly, and in 1866,
Montpellier, this drawing being a study for the Chantilly painting. It varies from the painted composition
in numerous respects and would have been executed in
1807, according to Lapauze.

A.C.

Jean-Auguste Dominique INGRES

29 The Stamaty Family

(La Famille Stamaty)

Lead pencil
18¼ by 14⅝ in. (46.3 by 37.1 cm.)
Signed and dated at lower right in lead pencil: *J.A. Ingres del. Roma 1818*

Louvre - No. RF 4114

This admirable drawing, which shows great intensity and a precise, sensitive graphic technique, depicts the members of a family whose acquaintance Ingres had made in Rome and with whom he maintained a strong friendship. One of the daughters, Atala, goddaughter of Chateaubriand, took her first painting lessons with the young artist.

A.C.

J. A. Ingres Del. Rom.
1818.

Jean-Auguste Dominique INGRES

30 Ossian's Dream

(Le Songe d'Ossian)

Lead pencil, pen, water color, heightened with white,
on tracing paper
10¼ by 8⅜ in. (26 by 21.2 cm.)
Signed and dated at lower left in pen and ink: *Ingres
inv. et pinx. Roma in Edibus Montecaval. 1812*

Louvre - No. RF 1446

In 1811 Ingres received the commission for a painting
which was supposed to decorate the ceiling of the Emperor's bedchamber in the Quirinal Palace and which
is now in the Musée de Montauban. Despite the date
on the bottom of the page, it seems that the execution
of the drawing in the Louvre would be placed at
about 1835-41, at the time when Ingres was thinking
of repairing the canvas, and in particular of squaring
it off, as its original form followed the oval of the
ceiling.

A.C.

Jean-Auguste Dominique INGRES

31 Portrait of Monsieur Leblanc

Lead pencil
18 by 14 in. (45.7 by 35.5 cm.)
Signed at lower left in lead pencil: *Ingres Del. à Madame Leblanc*
Dated at lower right in lead pencil: *Florence 9 Mars 1823*

Louvre - No. RF 5642

It was in the course of his stay in Florence (1820-24) that Ingres made the acquaintance of M. and Mme. Leblanc, whose portraits (half-length) he painted in 1822 and 1823, New York, Metropolitan Museum. The Musée de Montauban owns several drawings of M. or Mme. Leblanc which also relate to the paintings.

A.C.

Jean-Auguste Dominique INGRES

32   Portrait of Madame Devauçay

Brush and brown wash, lead pencil.
4½ by 3⅜ in. (11.3 by 8.7 cm.)
Signed at lower right in lead pencil: *Ingres.* Inscription
below, on the mount, in lead pencil: *à Madame Coutan*

Louvre - No. RF 1443

Mme. Devauçay was a Neapolitan, the mistress of the
French Ambassador Alquier, and was one of the women
who was most in the public eye in Rome around 1807,
at the time when Ingres painted her portrait, Chantilly,
Musée Condé. Besides the study in the Louvre there
are two drawings relating to the painting in the Ingres
Museum in Montauban, and a third in the Petit Palais.

A.C.

Jean-Auguste Dominique INGRES

33 **Study of a Nude Female Figure**

(Etude de femme nue)

Lead pencil
3⅞ by 6⅞ in. (9.8 by 17.6 cm.)

Louvre - No. RF 1095

The composition and the style of this drawing relate it
to the *Nude Woman Sleeping* (*Femme nue dormant*),
also called *The Sleeping Woman of Naples* (*La Dor-
meuse de Naples*), a painting which was bought by
Murat in 1809 and which disappeared after 1814.

A.C.

Jean-Auguste Dominique INGRES

34 Portrait of Monsieur Lavergne

Lead pencil
11 by 8⅝ in. (28 by 22 cm.)
Signed and dated lower left in lead pencil: *Ingres à Madame Lavergne Rome 1818*

Paris, Musée du Petit Palais
Duthuit Collection - No. 1156

According to information furnished by the painter R. Balze, a pupil of Ingres, Monsieur Lavergne was "equerry of king Charles IV of Spain." It was on the occasion of his first visit to Rome that Ingres painted this portrait, as well as that of Madame Lavergne, also kept at the Petit-Palais. Two other portrait drawings of Monsieur Lavergne are known: one, signed and dated 1830, is at the Musée Bonnat in Bayonne; the other at the Albertina in Vienna.

A.C.

Antoine-Jean GROS (Baron) Paris 1771 - Paris 1835

Gros' tragedy lay in his being unable to surmount the lifelong contradiction posed by the fact that he was David's favorite pupil, and yet was an impassioned supporter of the young Delacroix. He was the son of the miniature painter Jean-Antoine Gros, at the age of fourteen was admitted to David's studio, and in 1792 competed for the *Prix de Rome* but lost to Landon. He became suspect during the Revolution and decided to go to Italy, reaching Genoa a year later, after many difficulties. He went on to Florence, but it was in Genoa that he later met Josephine Bonaparte, who took him to Milan and presented him to her husband. From then on the destiny of this artist was to be tied to that of the hero, whose legendary silhouette Gros painted the day after the victory of Arcole in a brilliant rapid sketch (1796, Louvre). The following year Gros became Commissioner in charge of choosing works to enrich the Louvre, and, sharing the life of Napoleon's soldiers, he travelled around Italy from Milan to Venice and from Venice to Rome, where in the Sistine Chapel he experienced the revelation of the power of Michelangelo. He returned to France after an absence of eight years, hesitating still between David's doctrines of line and his own interest in the dynamics of color. Gros received the commission for a painting representing *The Battle of Nazareth* (*Le Combat de Nazareth*), 1801, sketch in the Musée de Nantes, a grandiose undertaking which was followed by *The Plague-Ridden People of Jaffa* (*Les Pestiférés de Jaffa*), 1804, Louvre, *The Battle of Aboukir*, 1806, Versailles, and *The Battle of Eylau*, 1808, Louvre, in which he established himself as an historical painter and as the bard of the Napoleonic period at its zenith. About 1812 he was commissioned to do the paintings for the dome of Sainte Geneviève, which he finished in 1824 and which earned him the title of Baron. Though the Restoration inspired other fine works from Gros: *The Departure of Louis XVIII for the Tuileries* (*Le Départ de Louis XVIII aux Tuileries*), 1817, Versailles, *The Embarcation of the Duchess of Angoulême* (*l'Embarquement de la Duchesse d'Angoulême*), 1819, Bordeaux, his epic and dramatic flair diminished during that time. Divided between a desire to pursue the work of his master David, and an equally strong need to abandon himself to the passions of his own temperament, Gros soon found himself condemned both by the newly-triumphant Romantics and by the Classicists who had re-assembled around Ingres. The criticisms which were levelled at his last composition (*Hercules and Diomedes*, 1835, Toulouse) threw him into profound despair and led him to suicide. On July 26, 1835 he drowned himself in the Seine at Bas-Meudon. It was a romantic death, and ironically one could say that by that time the prevalence of Romanticism in art had been prepared for by Gros himself—by his feeling for mass, for movement, and for color.

A.C.

35 Equestrian Portrait of Prince Joachim Murat

(Portrait équestre du Prince Joachim Murat)

Pen and ink, chalk
16 by 11½ in. (40.5 by 29.2 cm.)
Inscription in pen and ink at lower margin: « *Voilà à peu près la tournure que l'on peut donner au costume, d'après ce que l'on dit. A l'armée, le prince laisse croître ses moustaches. Quand vous en serez à la ressemblance, je vous prêterai un petit portrait commencé d'après nature. Girodet, à qui je l'ai prêté, me le rendra bientôt et je vous l'enverrai.* »
("Here more or less is the way the costume can be presented, according to what we have heard. In the army the Prince lets his moustaches grow. When you get to the likeness, I will lend you a little portrait which was begun from nature. Girodet, to whom I lent it, will give it back to me soon and I will send it on to you.")

Paris, Ecole des Beaux-Arts, No. 1054

Study for *The Battle of Eylau,* exhibited in the Salon of 1808 and now in the Louvre.

A.C.

François-Marius GRANET Aix-en-Provence 1775 - Rome 1849

Granet was the son of a master mason and received his first training in the studio of the landscape painter Constantin. There he made the acquaintance of Auguste de Forbin whose inseparable friend he soon became and whom he rejoined in Paris some years later. Thanks to Forbin he was admitted to the studio of David, at which time he lived with Ingres and a group of David's other students in the disaffected Capuchin monastery. In 1799 he submitted *The Little Cloister of the Feuillants* (*Le petit cloître des Feuillants*) to the Salon, where it met with critical acclaim. Three years later he went to Italy with Forbin and discovered Rome, which was to become a second native city for him. After an initial visit of twenty-two years he returned frequently and produced numerous painting which he sent to the Paris expositions and which enjoyed a well-deserved success: *The Underground Passages of Santa Maria in Via Lata* (*Les Souterrains de Santa Maria in Via Lata*), 1808, *Stella, the French Painter, in the Prisons of Rome* (*Stella, peintre français, dans les prisons de Rome*), 1810, or *The Capuchin Choir of the Barberini Church* (*Le Chœur des Capucins de l'Eglise Barberini*), Leningrad, Hermitage. This last painting was presented in the Salon of 1819 and aroused the enthusiasm of visitors to such an extent that the artist had to reproduce it more than fifteen times and it earned him the decoration of the Légion d'Honneur. Returning to Rome, Granet continued to paint churches and convents, sending to the Salon of 1822 an *Interior of the Lower Church in Assisi*, Louvre, and then in 1824 *Domenichino at the Villa Aldobrandini* (*Le Dominiquin à la villa Aldobrandini*). Recalled to Paris by Forbin, who in 1824 had been named Associate Curator of the Royal Museums, then Curator, Granet had difficulty becoming used to the climate of Paris, and in 1829 went back to Rome for several months. Then in 1830 he finally returned to France for good, but even though he was patronized by Louis-Philippe who gave him numerous commissions, Granet no longer had the popular public recognition he had had earlier. After the death of his wife in 1847 he retired to Aix-en-Provence where he continued to work very hard. When he died, on November 21, 1849, he left to his native city most of his belongings, works and collections, except for two hundred drawings which he gave to the Louvre.

A.C.

36 Persons Gathered in a Crypt

(Personnages assemblés dans une crypte)

Brush and brown wash
6⅞ by 9⅝ in. (17.5 by 24.5 cm.)
Inscription below in the artist's hand: *Croquis de mon tableau d'Ernani* (sic). ("Sketch of my Hernani painting") (sic)
Inscription above in another hand: *Envoyé par Granet dans une lettre à son ami M. Paulin du Queylard à Valmontre.* ("Sent by Granet in a letter to his friend M. Paulin du Queylard in Valmontre.")

Paris, Musée du Petit Palais, No. 1207

Granet was engrossed by the problem of light which he considered to be the chief element of painting, and his wash drawings exhibit the most subtle nuances of light and shadow. Prime importance in this composition is given to effects of chiaroscuro, and the vigorous oppositions which the artist produced here provides a characteristic example of the originality of his talent. The first performance of Victor Hugo's celebrated play took place in Paris in 1830, which permits us to date this drawing thereabouts; furthermore, after 1830 Granet abandoned wash in favor of water color.

A.C.

Théodore GÉRICAULT Rouen 1791 - Paris 1824

From his youth Géricault devoted himself to his two passions: horsemanship and painting. In 1808, then aged seventeen, he entered Carle Vernet's studio, and in 1810 that of Guérin. He had greatest admiration, however, for Gros, because Gros recognized in him a kindred heroic fervor and encouraged him strongly. In the Salon of 1812 Géricault exhibited a large painting, *Officier de Chasseurs*, followed in 1814 by its companion-piece, *The Wounded Cavalryman* (*Le Cuirassier blessé*); then when he was twenty-five years old, he left for Italy. The drawings from his Italian period are characterized by the expressive power of their workmanship and by their great dynamic quality. They reflect a double concern on the part of the artist: depictions of scenes observed in everyday life on one hand, and rediscovery of antiquity through its sculpture on the other. When Géricault returned, he made many sketches and studies for his *Raft of the Medusa* of 1819. His voyage to England in 1820-21 brought new elements into his work such as the re-creation of the instantaneousness of reality, this being admirably achieved in his *Epsom Derby* in the Louvre. Two years after he returned from England, Géricault died as the result of a fall from a horse. He was only thirty-three.

G.M.

37 Thoroughbred

(Pur-Sang)

Water color, heightened with gouache, over black chalk
9⅝ by 12¼ in. (24.4 by 31 cm.)

Louvre — No. RF 803

The type of horse, and the use of water color as the essential medium of the drawing, seem to suggest that this is a study done during Géricault's stay in England (1820-21). It fits in with a whole series of water colors representing horses and grooms, or horsemen promenading, which were strongly influenced by contemporary English lithographs. The same influence is also evident in his celebrated painting, *The Epsom Derby*, now in the Louvre.

G.M.

Théodore GERICAULT

38 Ancient Sacrifice

(Sacrifice Antique)

Pen and brown ink, heightened with gouache, on oiled
paper
9¼ by 15¾ in. (23.5 by 40.2 cm.)

Louvre — No. RF 417

The dramatic power of this drawing with its large
format is accentuated by its contrasts of vivid light,
achieved by white highlights on the dark background
of the paper. There is also strong expressive violence in
the scene itself of executioners beating their cowering
beasts. The drawing is characteristic of Géricault's Italian period in that it reveals his double concern for
recalling an actual scene which he could well have
witnessed in the beef markets, and at the same time
drawing something reminiscent of the numerous ancient
bas-reliefs which he copied in Italy from 1816-17.

G.M.

Théodore GERICAULT

39   The Hunt
(La Chasse)

Pen and ink, gray wash, heightened with white, over
black chalk, on brown paper
7⅞ by 8⅞ in. (18.9 by 22.5 cm.)
Signed and dated at lower right in pen and ink: *Géricault Rome 1817*

Louvre — No. 1749

This horseman chasing a deer is presented in the ancient
manner and is a characteristic example of Géricault's
drawing style during his stay in Rome. It is not only
clearly reminiscent of hunting scenes on antique sarco-
phagi, but also reflects the influence of Michelangelo in
its particularly dynamic style. The sense of modelling
and movement and the manner in which Géricault has
handled the highlighted wash create a strong kinship
between this drawing and two of the following (Nos.
40 and 42).

G.M.

Théodore GERICAULT

40 Centaur Abducting a Nymph
(Centaure enlevant une nymphe)

Pen and ink, gray wash, heightened with white, on oiled paper
6⅞ by 8⅞ in. (17.5 by 22.5 cm.)

Louvre — No. 26737

This vigorous study belongs, as does the preceding one, to Géricault's Roman period, but it evokes even more, perhaps, a group sculpted in high relief, in that its oppositions of light and shadow accentuate the impression of relief. We see the nervous, energetic quality of Géricault the draughtsman revealed in the pen and Indian ink technique which permitted him great rapidity of execution.

G.M.

Théodore GERICAULT

41 Combat Between Horsemen
(Combat des cavaliers)

Brush and gray wash, water color, heightened with white, over black chalk, on brown paper
7½ by 10⅝ in. (19 by 27 cm.)

Louvre — No. RF 834

This wash drawing has a romantic character and depicts one episode from the Madagascar war in which the soldiers of the Empire confronted the Mameluks. The subject served as inspiration for several of Géricault's sketches—most notably a drawing in the Louvre (No. RF 796) which Charles Clément, the author of the 1879 published catalogue of Géricault's work, situated between 1812 and 1816. One sees in such compositions that there was a patriotic impulse common to the artists of this generation—Gros and Girodet, for example—who were almost all trained in David's studio.

G.M.

Théodore GERICAULT

42 Faun and Nymph

(Faune et nymphe)

Black chalk, brush and gray wash, heightened with
white on buff paper
7⅜ by 9¼ in. (18.7 by 23.7 cm.)

Louvre — No. RF 851

Still allied to the group of drawings executed during
the artist's stay in Rome, in that the composition focusses
on a sculptured group of figures, this drawing, however,
does exhibit other tendencies in Géricault's manner of
treating mythological subjects. There is a more gentle,
gliding way of handling the stumped black chalk, and
the general climate of the scene is more sentimental. He
has unfolded it within the framework of landscape,
according to a formula which was used quite often at
the opening of the century—by an artist like Prud'hon
for example.

G.M.

Théodore GERICAULT

43 Cavalier

Brush and gray wash, water color, over lead pencil
10¼ by 9 in. (26 by 23 cm.)
Signed at lower left in chalk: *Géricault.* At lower right
in pen: *Géricault*

Paris, Ecole des Beaux-Arts, No. 996

Typical of Géricault's youthful graphic style when he
was impassioned by equestrian subjects, this water color
reflects the work of his master Carle Vernet and is dated
between 1812 and 1816 by Charles Clément. It belonged (as did Nos. 42 and 45) to the celebrated collector His de la Salle, who, being a Lieutenant of the Imperial Guard himself, particularly appreciated Géricault's
military and equestrian subjects and collected a great
number of his drawings and prints.

G.M.

Théodore GERICAULT

44 The Slave Trade

(La traite des nègres)

Red chalk, pen and brown ink, on grey paper
12⅛ by 17⅛ in. (30.7 by 43.6 cm.)

Paris, Ecole des Beaux-Arts, No. 982

This red chalk drawing with its nervous additions in pen
represents one of the last of Géricault's works, being
one of the ensemble sketches for an extremely large
canvas which he never executed, but toward which he
was working from 1823 until his death. The rapid pen
drawing of the same subject, now in the Musée Bonnat in Bayonne, is generally considered to have been
his initial work on the project. The abolition of slavery
did not occur until 1848, so it was one of the burning
questions of the time. Géricault has treated it here with
passion, though his nervous energy is tempered by his
use of line which emphatically defines the contours of
the numerous figures.

G.M.

Théodore GERICAULT

45 Full-Length Portrait
of an Officer of the Carabiniers

(Officier de Carabiniers vu en pied)

Pen and brown ink, water color, over lead pencil lines
15⅜ by 12¼ in. (39 by 31 cm.)

Louvre — No. RF 799

This large drawing is an early work and in fact shows
a certain stiffness in its execution and its somewhat hard
outlining of the contours. But it shows Géricault's
consistently live interest in real-life subjects, particularly
those which concerned the Imperial Army, and it is
reminiscent of his studies for the painting he presented
at the Salon of 1812 *Officier de chasseurs*, to which *The
Wounded Cavalryman* (*Le Cuirassier blessé*), Louvre,
shown at the 1814 Salon was a companion piece.

G.M.

Eugène DELACROIX Saint-Maurice 1798 - Paris 1863

Delacroix' great stature both as a man and as an artist made him one of the dominating figures of his time; there was not a single strong experimental step taken in painting which was not presaged and heralded by him. He was born in Saint-Maurice, near Paris, on April 26, 1798, and as a very young child showed precocious tastes for drawing and for the theatre. After having received a solid classical education between 1806 and 1815, his numerous visits to the Louvre convinced him of his vocation. In the spring of 1816 he entered Guérin's studio, but he was rather hostile to the academicism taught by his master and paid most attention to the new impulse which Gros and Géricault were giving to painting. The passionate quality which animates *Dante's Boat* (*la Barque de Dante*), exhibited in the Salon of 1822, reveals to what point the art of those two masters had impressed him. His *Episodes from the Massacres of Scio* (*Scènes des Massacres de Scio*), Salon of 1824, Louvre, consummated the rupture between the two camps, Classical and Romantic, and caused a great scandal, but this painting rallied the young to Delacroix' side, and despite himself he became the leader of the new school. From the end of May to the end of August, 1825, he travelled in England, gaining from this trip a greater suppleness of technique and a deepened awareness of his literary and poetic sources. In 1827 when he returned, he exhibited his "massacre No. 2", *The Death of Sardanapale* (*la Mort de Sardanapale*), Louvre, a painting which had been inspired by Byron, and which unleashed all the fury of the critics at its audacity. Three years later Delacroix produced *Liberty Leading The People*, Louvre, which can be considered as the crowning conclusion and summation of his romantic youth, and which marked him unquestionably as the successor to Gros and Géricault, though his range was far greater than theirs. The year 1831 brought a decisive turning point in his career: he accompanied the Count de Mornay on a mission to the Sultan of Morocco, and for the artist, this journey was not only a revelation of classical antiquity, but of the full magic of colors and light. All his life he was to remain imbued with the remembrance of the voyage, and he worked incessantly from the notes and sketches he had made at that time. His return brought on an intense period of activity: he became involved in a ceaseless program of mural decorations which occupied him until his death, and he continued to remain in the public eye by producing more and more numerous paintings. This period saw the creation of Delacroix' most beautiful masterpieces: *Women of Algiers*, 1834, Louvre, *The Entry of the Crusaders Into Constantinople* (*L'Entrée des Croisés à Constantinople*), 1840, Louvre, as well as the decorations of the Palais Bourbon, the Palais du Luxembourg, and of the ceiling of the Galerie d'Apollon, Louvre. He retired from the world more and more in order to devote himself entirely to his work, for he was gravely attacked by illness as he grew older. Finally Delacroix gave over his spiritual will and testament to the walls of Saint-Sulpice before dying in his studio in the Place de Furstenberg on August 13, 1863.

A.C.

46 Portrait of a Young Woman
(Portrait de jeune femme)

Pen and ink
3⅞ by 3⅝ in. (9.8 by 9.3 cm.)

Louvre — No. RF 9220

Alfred Robaut, the biographer of Delacroix who owned this drawing, dated it *circa* 1826: "Here," he says, "is one of those lively sketches in which Delacroix expressed the synthesis of a face in just a few lines of his pen . . .".

A.C.

Eugène DELACROIX

A.C.

47 **Three Horses Rearing**

(Trois chevaux cabrés)

Black chalk, heightened with white, on beige paper
8¼ by 11¼ in. (21 by 28.5 cm.)
On the verso, studies of horses and of a head, in the
same technique

Louvre — No. RF 16.293

The dynamic graphic quality of these studies and the
fact that they are so reminiscent of Géricault permit us
to place them around 1823-25, the period during which
Delacroix made so many sketches of horses from
nature.

A.C.

Eugène DELACROIX

48 Paolo and Francesca

Water color
11 by 8¼ in. (28 by 21 cm.)
Signed at lower right: *Eug. Delacroix*

Collection of Dr. Peter Nathan, Zurich

Inspired by the Fifth Canto of Dante's *Inferno*, this
water color, in its transparency and its supple execution,
show the influence of English water colorists such as
Thales Fielding, who was a friend of Delacroix. It
would therefore probably have been painted in 1824
or 1825.

A.C.

Eugène DELACROIX

49 **Study of a Child**
(Etude d'enfant)

Black chalk, heightened with white, on grey-brown
paper
17¼ by 10¾ in. (43.7 by 27.4 cm.)
Inscriptions at lower right in chalk in the artist's hand:
*Mad. Louis cul de sac d'Amboise no. 1 près de la place
Maubert*
Below: *la Vierge*
Below, in an unknown hand: *Bristol bleuté filet or
dessus et teinté*
Mark of the sale after Delacroix' death at the lower
right.

Louvre — No. RF 9162

This study was executed for the figure of the Infant
Jesus in the *Virgin of the Harvesters* (*Vierge des Mois-
sons*), the first commission which Delacroix received
(in 1819) for the church in the little village of Orcemont,
where it still remains today. As the note written by the
artist himself on the drawing indicates, this was a
little girl from the Place Maubert whom he used as
a model.

                                                    A.C.

Eugène DELACROIX

50 Negro in a Turban
(Nègre au turban)

Pastel
18½ by 14¾ in. (47 by 37.5 cm.)

Louvre — No. A D 24

According to M. Escholier, this very beautiful pastel is
a study for the Turk on horseback in *The Massacres
of Scio*, executed around 1824. Delacroix was extremely
interested in pastel technique and used it several times
during his career. In his journal one finds various notes
concerning methods of fixing it.

A.C.

Eugène DELACROIX

51 Portrait of Monsieur Pierret's Mother
(Portrait de Madame Pierret mère)

Lead pencil
9¾ by 8½ in. (25 by 21.8 cm.)
Dated at lower right in the artist's hand: *13 Avril vendredi Saint, 1827*

Boymans van Beuningen Museum, Rotterdam.

Delacroix' friendship for the various members of the
family of his childhood friend, J.B. Pierret, is evident
in this portrait of the latter's wife, executed with great
seriousness and extreme sensitivity. The artist made
numerous sketches of this young woman, and it was her
nervous, profound face which was the inspiration for his
figure of Hamlet.

A.C.

13 avril Vendredi fa~
1827

Victor HUGO Paris 1802 - 1885

While it is not at all rare that on the margins, as it were, of their literary creativity poets and writers should often have turned to plastic media for expression, few of them have ever surpassed the visionary genius of Victor Hugo or equalled his magnificent improvisations which, according to Théophile Gautier "mix Goya's chiaroscuro effects with Piranesi's architectural terror." A born draughtsman who resembled nobody else, even though he brings other masters to mind, Victor Hugo was already drawing in his notebooks as a schoolboy and when he was not conjuring up the invisible, his insatiable curiosity was feeding intensively on whatever he saw. He was an "amateur" who never had any teaching, but perhaps because of this he invented procedures whose bizarre quality often escapes analysis: strange techniques (touches of ink, foldings, cut-outs) and un-orthodox materials (pen feathers, coal, soot, which he alternated with sepia, wash, pen or charcoal). His drawings show an astonishing variety—both reflecting whatever work he had in progress, such as those which illustrate *The Toilers of the Sea* (*les Travailleurs de la mer*) or *The Rhine*, and prefiguring his later writings. They were often done as souvenirs of his travels: from tragic mountains on the banks of the Rhine, ruins in Flanders, or Swiss landscapes, to revelations of Baroque art or architecture. These drawings also apprehend things which lie hidden in the deep abysses of the spirit: strange things which reached inordinate proportions through the monstrous, fantastic creatures, the fierce and somber fantasies of Victor Hugo the Romantic poet. In the words of Elie Faure, he "found the summit of his expression with blazing sureness in the object."

L.D.

52 View of a German Town
(Vue d'une ville allemande)

Pen, gray and brown wash, water color
12⅜ by 19⅜ in. (31.4 by 49.1 cm.)
Signed at lower right in a brush and wash: *Victor Hugo*
Inscription below in pen and ink: *pour toi, mon Charles - 1866*

Louvre — No. RF 12188

This magnificent drawing, dedicated to the artist's grandson, is an excellent example of the twilight atmosphere and fevered style characteristic of Victor Hugo's graphic work. We are reminded, furthermore, that it was the Romantics who restored the Middle Ages to popular recognition by deriving inspiration from its architecture.

A.C.

Victor HUGO

53   **Reclining Nude Female Figure,
Seen from the Back**

("Sub clara nuda lucerna")

Pen and ink, wash
6⅜ by 11 in. (17 by 28 cm.)

Paris, Maison de Victor Hugo, No. 264

The latin quotation "Nude under the clear light of
the lamp" from Horace is found in different contexts
in Victor Hugo's Notebooks, and this drawing shows
his habit of observing the intimate moments of servants.
Gaëtan Picon finds in "the foreshortening of the left
arm and the almost straight line of the profile ... the
coherent and allusive distortions of Picasso." (*Victor
Hugo dessinateur,* Editions du Minotaure, 1963, note
No. 229 and Preface, p. 14).

L.D.

SVB CLARÂ NVDA LVCERNÂ

Victor HUGO

54   The Tower of Rats

(La Tour des Rats)

Pen and ink, brown wash
11 by 16⅞ in. (28 by 43 cm.)
Signed and dated at lower right: *27 7bre 1840, La Tour des Rats, Victor H.*

Paris, Maison de Victor Hugo, No. 49

In *The Rhine* Victor Hugo has described his visit to this place which haunted his childhood and tells the legend of Archbishop Hatto who was devoured by the rats in the tower where he had taken refuge. (*Victor Hugo dessinateur*, Editions du Minotaure, 1963, excerpt from Note No. 34).

L.D.

Antoine Louis BARYE Paris 1796 - Paris 1875

Barye, who was without doubt the greatest animal sculptor since the Assyrians, was equally good as a painter. Long-accustomed to working with a chisel, having studied sculpture with Bosio, he also had studied painting with Gros and he obtained First Prize in the Sketching Competition of 1823 with *The Quarrel Between Hector and Paris* (*les Reproches d'Hector et de Pâris*). Subsequently, however, he deliberately abandoned his study of the human figure to analyze the world of beasts. He entered the employ of the goldsmith Fauconnier as a worker, but spent all his free time in the Jardin des Plantes producing innumerable tracing and sketches to which he continued to add, as documentary repertoire, all his life. After 1849 Barye often visited his friends Millet, Rousseau and Diaz in Barbizon, where he worked from nature and explored the possibilities of those harsh and highly colored natural settings which he created for the games and combats of his wild beasts. In 1854 he was named Professor of Zoological Drawing at the Museum of Natural History, and the same contained force which gives life to his bronzes can be felt in his numerous water colors. They hold a position of prime importance in the evolution of French drawing in the nineteenth century through their evocation of landscape and through the true rendering and the beauty of Barye's animals.

A.C.

55 Tiger Lying in Wait
(Tigre à l'affût)

Water color
10⅜ by 14¾ in. (26.5 by 37.4 cm.)
Signed at lower left: *Barye*

Montpellier, Musée Fabre, No. 876-3-96

"Force, suppleness, ferocity and hunger conspire with solitude." Théophile Silvestre's comment justly calls attention to the imperious and ferocious character of this superb beast whose apparently nonchalant walk hides the dormant streak of lightning which he is building up.

A.C.

Nicolas-Toussaint CHARLET Paris 1792 - 1845

Charlet, whose origins were humble, began work as an
employee in the mayor's office before entering the studio
of Gros at the age of twenty-five. The pupil and the
master had their strong admiration for Bonaparte in
common, and very quickly Charlet began to specialize in
military scenes inspired by the numerous campaigns of
the Consulate and of the Empire. He was equally interested in scenes of everyday life as he observed them
first hand in the streets of Paris. He was essentially a
draughtsman and lithographer, and the realism of his
subjects, which he often accompanied with humorous
comments, makes him a herald of that whole current
of artists such as Raffet, Daumier, Gavarni, Forain, whose
satirical verve was to become an important theme of the
second half of the nineteenth century.

G.M.

56 The Boules Players

(Les Joueurs de Boules)

Pen and brown ink, brown wash
13¾ by 18⅛ in. (35 by 46 cm.)
Signed at lower right in brush and wash: *Charlet*

Paris, Musée des Arts Décoratifs, No. 23888

Though the tone of this street scene is picturesque, it is
strengthened by Charlet's realistic study of the people,
whose gestures are eloquent and whose faces are ren-
dered almost as caricature masks.

G.M.

Jean-Baptiste CARPEAUX Valenciennes 1827 - Courbevoie (Seine) 1875

Carpeaux was both a painter and a sculptor. He came to Paris in 1842, three years later entered the studio of François Rude, and obtained the *Prix de Rome* for sculpture in 1854 so that he was then a fellow at the Villa Medici from 1856 to January, 1862. There he executed the plaster cast of *Ugolin*, which was exhibited as a bronze in Paris at the Salon of 1863. When Carpeaux returned to Paris he was presented to Princess Mathilde, who in turn introduced him at the Imperial Court, where he soon became the official sculptor. He then made numerous busts and many sketches depicting the Court festivities. His large commissions were the decoration of the Pavillon de Flore at the Louvre, the group *La Danse* for the façade of the Paris Opera, and the Fountain in the Observatory. Carpeaux' rendering of movement and light in his black chalk or pastel drawings makes it clear that his vision came very close to that of the Impressionists.

G.M.

57 Head of an Arab

(Tête d'Arabe)

Brush and brown wash
7¾ by 5⅛ in. (19.8 by 13 cm.)
Inscription at lower right in chalk: *4*

Louvre - No. RF 1218
This study relates to a bas relief entitled *The Submission of Abd-el-Kader* (*La Soumission d'Abd-el-Kader*) which depicts the interview between Abd-el-Kader and Napoleon III. The plaster cast, which was finished in 1853 and was exhibited that same year at the Salon, is now in the Musée de Versailles, while the marble, which was executed a little later, belongs to the Musée de Valenciennes. The vigorous use of brush in this drawing bears witness to the rapidity with which Carpeaux executed portraits of this kind.

G.M.

4

Constantin GUYS Flessingue 1808 - Paris 1892

Though he was essentially a draughtsman, Constantin Guys led a most vagabond existence. He served as a soldier with Lord Byron in Greece during the War of Independence (1823). In 1848 he became war correspondent for The Illustrated London News, which meant that he was present at the scene of several important historical events, notably the Revolution of 1848 and the Crimean War (1853-1855). After travelling throughout all of Europe and in the Orient he finally established himself in Paris around 1862, devoting himself entirely to drawing, with absolutely no desire for profit and with a horror of any publicity.

"A genius for whom no aspect of life is uninteresting" (Baudelaire), gifted with tireless curiosity, Constantin Guys was as aware of brilliant festivities, elegant uniforms, or the details in a dress, as he was perceptive about the ugliness and perversities of the poorer sections of Paris. He provides us with a faithful reflection of life under the Second Empire. But while his drawings have left us the image of a society, they also illustrate above all Guys' personal search for "that something-or-other which we may be permitted to call modernity . . . ," his concern for "sifting out of Fashion whatever she may contain of poetry in the midst of history—for separating the eternal from the transitory." (Baudelaire)

A.C.

58 **Young Woman in a Full Blue Skirt**

(Jeune Femme en crinoline bleue)

Watercolor heightened with gouache
12¼ x 8⅜ in. (31.0 x 22.0 cm.)

Paris, Musée du Petit-Palais, No. 1525-5

Constantin GUYS

59 Girls Dancing in a Cabaret

(Filles dansant dans un cabaret)

Pen and black ink, gray wash

Paris, Musée du Petit Palais, No. 1540

Guys was not afraid to depict the popular clientele of the Bal Mabille or the Closerie des Lilas as well as his "dandys" and "women of the world"; his brush suggests more than it draws, and thanks to his remarkably acute observation we completely feel the rather lifeless atmosphere of this cabaret.

A.C.

Constantin GUYS

60 Young Woman in a Blue Bonnet with a Fan

(Jeune femme au cabriolet bleu et à l'éventail)

Water color and gray wash
8⅝ x 5⅞ in. (22.0 x 15.0 cm.)

Paris, Musée du Petit-Palais, No. 1524

In this splendid water color with its contrasting tones Guys reveals himself as a connoisseur of fashion and elegance but also as the painter par excellence of women. Through the virtuosity and finesse of his brush he stands as the response to Baudelaire's questions: "What poet, in painting the pleasure caused by the apparition of a beauty, would dare separate the woman from her costume? Where is there a man who, in the street, at the theatre, in the park, has not been delighted in a completely disinterested way by a scrupulously accomplished toilette, but has not carried away with it in his mind an inseparable image of the beauty of the person to whom it belonged, thus making the two, the woman and her dress, into an indivisible whole?"

A.C.

Constantin GUYS

61 **Hussars at Table with Several Girls**
(Hussards attablés avec des filles)

Pen and ink, water color, over chalk
8⅞ x 13¾ in. (22.5 x 35.0 cm.)

Musée du Petit Palais, Paris — No. 1536

A clearly ordered composition, using rather washed-out
water color, in which Guys has treated the old theme of
"girl and soldier" in an extremely simple but at the
same time very suggestive manner.

A.C.

Théodore CHASSÉRIAU Ste. Barbe de Samana (Santo Domingo) 1819 - Paris 1856

Chassériau was born in the Antilles, of French parents, his father being then the French Consul on Saint Thomas. He came to Paris at an early age and entered Ingres' studio in 1833, quickly becoming the master's favorite pupil. The influence on Chassériau of his first teacher is noticeable in the very linear rhythm of his 1838 painting, *Vénus Marine*. In 1840 he left Paris in order to join Ingres in Rome, and there he executed the painted portrait of R.P. Lacordaire which was exhibited at the Salon of 1841 and is now in the Louvre. *Esther Preparing for her Presentation to King Ahasuerus* (*Esther se parant pour être presentée au Roi Assuerus*) dated 1841, and *The Two Sisters* (*Les Deux Sœurs*) dated 1843 (both in the Louvre) show that his style had already reached its maturity. In 1846, following the example of Delacroix, whose highly colored palette he admired, Chassériau travelled to Algeria, bringing back many precious water color sketches. When he was back in Paris, he received a commission to paint large decorative frescoes for the Church of St. Roch and for the Cour des Comptes, of which some fragments escaped the destruction of 1871 and are now in the Louvre. The monumentality of his style paved the way directly for the art of Gustave Moreau and Puvis de Chavannes.

G.M.

62 Portrait of Lord Lytton

Lead pencil
12¼ x 9½ in. (31.2 x 24.0 cm.)
Signed and date at lower right in lead pencil: *Th. Chassériau Avril 1851*

Louvre - No. RF 24376

Even Chassériau's earliest works, the portraits of his brother Frédéric and his sisters Adèle and Aline, done around 1834-35, reveal his mastery of portraiture. While he adopted the precise, detailed lead pencil technique previously used by Ingres, Chassériau went beyond his master in seeking to express the interior personality of his models, to whom he often gave pensive expressions. This portrait of the English ambassador to France —a diplomat, as was the artist's father—is dated 1851 and reveals great ease and ability in its execution.

G.M.

Ch. Chassériau
Avril 1851

Théodore CHASSERIAU

63 **Study of a Nude Female Figure:
Odalisque**

(Etude de nue: Odalisque)

Lead pencil
2¾ x 4⅞ in. (7.0 x 12.4 cm.)
Signed at lower left in lead pencil: *Th. Chassériau*

Louvre, No. RF 24434

This nude is delicate and restrained in its execution and
is still very close to the works preceding Chassériau's
voyage to Italy, such as the *Vénus Marine* of 1838. The
subject itself and the linear treatment of it, echo the
work of his master Ingres, whose *Odalisque*, now in the
Louvre, is dated 1814.

G.M.

Théodore CHASSERIAU

64 Arabs of Algiers

(Arabes d'Alger)

Brush and brown wash, water color, over lead pencil
14¼ x 10⅞ in. (36.2 x 27.7 cm.)
At upper left notes in the artist's hand imitating Arab
characters, and below in brush: *Hussein Osman*

Louvre - No. 243454

Chassériau left Paris May 3, 1846, and arrived in Marseilles the 8th, embarking a short time later for Africa.
He went to Philippeville, then visited Constantine and
Algiers, and arrived back in Paris in mid-July. During
this trip he made a considerable number of notes in
the form of sketches and drawings, as Eugène Delacroix
had done in 1832 in Morocco and Algeria. This drawing was without doubt executed during that year (1846).

G.M.

Théodore CHASSERIAU

65 **Saint Mary Magdalen in the Desert**
(Sainte Madeleine dans le desert)

Pen and brown ink, water color
8⅛ x 5¼ in. (20.6 x 13.5 cm.)
Inscription below at center in pen and brown ink : *Madeleine, Magdeleine*
At lower left stamp of the Chassériau sale

Louvre - No. 24.500

In a book about Chassériau, Léonce Benedite identifies this sheet as one of a group of twelve pen sketches executed for the prayer book of Madame de Ranchicourt, née Clotilde de Buns d'Hollebake, who had just married Chassériau's friend, M. de Ranchicourt, when the artist visited them in Lille during the summer of 1837. This would permit us to date this lively study at the outset of his career, before he went to Italy.

G.M.

SSERIAU

« Magdeleine »

Gustave MOREAU Paris 1826 - 1898

Gustave Moreau, the son of a Parisian architect, entered the studio of François Picot at the Ecole des Beaux-Arts in 1846. Two years later he assisted Théodore Chassériau in completing the frescoes which decorated the stairway of the old Cour des Comptes in Paris. The influence of this second master is therefore very important in the development of Moreau's style. His first participation in the Salon came in 1852 when he exhibited a *Pietà* which was bought by the government. In 1857 he went to Italy, where for two years he worked intensely at drawing, as can be seen by the numerous copies he made from the old masters. Soon after his return to Paris he began to accumulate studies for his celebrated painting *Oedipus and the Sphinx*, which is now in the Metropolitan Museum in New York. From then on he created one great painting after another on themes derived from many sources—chiefly Biblical and mythological: *Jason and Medea, The Young Man and Death (Jeune Homme et la Mort)* (1856), *Young Thracian Girl Carrying the Head of Orpheus (Jeune fille Thrace portant la tête d'Orphée)* (1866), *Prometheus* (1869), *Salome Dancing Before Herod (Salomé dansant devant Hérode)* (1876), *The Apparition* (1878), *Galatea* (1880). Gustave Moreau's work is essentially centered on the theme of Woman in her role as the evil heroine, such as Delilah or Salome. All his life he suffered the polemics of a great number of critics who saw him as nothing but a "literary painter," but his work was nevertheless sanctioned by official honors: in 1883 he was named an Officer of the Légion d'Honneur, in 1888 a member of the Academy of Fine Arts, and in 1892 professor at the Ecole des Beaux-Arts—a professor, furthermore, who was greatly loved and admired and whose loyal pupils included Rouault and Matisse. Desiring that "the sum total of his work and efforts" be kept undivided forever, Gustave Moreau decided to leave his town house and all its contents to the State after his death. There are some seven thousand drawings and three hundred paintings in this building (now the Musée Gustave Moreau) on Rue de la Rochefoucauld in Paris, bearing witness to Moreau's ceaseless work in producing countless sketches and studies in preparation for his great canvases. Linear treatment, and a sense of arabesque and harmonious contour are the most characteristic elements in his style. Even in the paintings in which his pictorial matière is richest, the style remains essentially graphic.

G.M.

66 The Woes of the Poet

(Les plaintes du poète)

Water color heightened with gold
11 x 6¾ in. (28.0 x 17.0 cm.)
Signed below in gold letters: *Gustave Moreau*
(Inscription: *Les Plaintes du Poète. Dessin pour émail*)
(The Woes of the Poet. Study for enamel)

Louvre - No. RF 12237

As the annotation in the artist's handwriting indicates, this water color is one of several which were to inspire enamel workers to reproduce Moreau's paintings. The chief among these enamelists were Frédéric de Courcy (whose rendering of *Oedipus and the Spinx* was exhibited in the 1866 Salon) Paul Grand'homme and Alfred Garnier. The latter two men, working together after 1888, are responsible for *The Young Man and Death (le Jeune Homme et la Mort)* enamel which is now in the Musée des Arts Décoratifs. Charles Hayem, who owned this water color, also had enamels in his collection, as we see from one of his letters written November 17, 1893: " ... at last I believe I now have found a setting for the enamels executed from your works."

G.M.

Gustave MOREAU

67 **Delilah**

(Dalila)

Water color
6¼ x 8⅜ in. (15.8 x 21.3 cm.)
Signed at lower right in water color: *Gustave Moreau*
Inscription at lower left in water color: *Dalila*

Louvre - No. RF 12386

This extremely competent water color, portraying a
theme which recurred often in Moreau's work after
1860, was commissioned by Charles Hayem who gave
his collection to the Musée Nationaux in 1898. It can
be dated much later than 1860 thanks to a letter of
June 7, 1882, addressed to the artist by the collector:
"I have just received your six first water colors: *Saint
Michael, Delilah, Sphinx, Giotto, Pietà* . . . "
The accent here is on rich color—justified of course by
the oriental decor and costumes—and strong emphasis
is placed on developing arabesques to tie the various
forms together. We note the artist's own formula: "To
evoke thought through the powers of line, arabesque
and plastic media, that is my aim."

G.M.

Gustave MOREAU

68 Study of a Seated Nude Female Figure

(Etude de nue: Femme assise)

Pen and black ink heightened with gouache
8⅝ x 12⅝ in. (22.0 x 32.0 cm.)
Squared in black chalk
Signed at lower right in black chalk: *Gustave Moreau*

Musée Gustave Moreau, Paris

Definitive study for the central figure in Moreau's large
painting entitled *Galatea*, which he exhibited in the
Salon of 1880 and which belonged to the Taigny collection. Another version, painted in a smaller format, is
now in the R. Lebel collection in Paris.
The very direct quality of this sketch indicates that it
was one of the studies Moreau did from a live model in
his studio; true to his customary method, once the
figure was transposed into the painting she became
more idealized.

G.M.

Gustave Moreau

Gustave MOREAU

69 Oedipus and the Sphinx
(Oedipe et le Sphinx)

Water color
14⅜ x 7½ in. (36.5 x 19.0 cm.)
Signed at lower left in water color: *Gustave Moreau*

Louvre - No. RF 2131

It was for his friend and fervent admirer Charles Hayem
that Gustave Moreau executed this version of his celebrated painting on the same subject which had made a
sensation at the 1864 Salon and which now hangs in
the Metropolitan Museum in New York. The con-
frontation of the man and the sphinx is emphasized by
extreme fixity of gesture set against a petrified background of blue mountains.

G.M.

Gustave MOREAU

70 Study of a Head

(Etude de tête)

Red chalk
8⅞ x 5½ in. (22.5 x 14.0 cm.)
Signed at lower left in red chalk: *Gustave Moreau*

Musée Gustave Moreau, Paris

Judging from numerous drawings in the Musée Gustave Moreau dated 1856, Moreau must have had an entirely personal predilection for the use of red chalk during that year. It is likely that this study with its bold modelling was also done at this time. It seems to be a free interpretation derived from antique sculpture, and it was from analogous motifs that Moreau eventually created the type of rather ambiguous, more and more stylized personage which became so characteristic in his work.

G.M.

Gustave MOREAU

71   Prometheus

Water color over lead pencil
10⅝ x 6⅜ in. (27.0 x 16.3 cm.)
Signed at lower left in water color: *Gustave Moreau*

Musée Gustave Moreau, Paris

This water color is similar in composition to the large painting of the same subject signed and dated 1868, exhibited in the Salon of 1869 and now in the Musée Gustave Moreau. The artist himself has explained the scene: " ... like a pilot keeping watch from the prow of his ship, he looks off into the distant icy spaces, sounding out the entire horizon, and smiling at his dream ... "

G.M.

Gustave MOREAU

72 Portrait of a Woman

(Portrait de femme)

Water color, pen and brown ink, heightened with white
gouache, over black chalk
7¾ x 5½ in. (19.7 x 14.0 cm.)

Musée Gustave Moreau, Paris

This delicate water color is without doubt one of the
rare portraits done from a live model that we have by
Moreau; it portrays one of the elegant society women of
the Second Empire. Moreau had been introduced at
Court, and we do know that he painted portraits of the
Emperor and Empress.

G.M.

Gustave MOREAU

73 Hercules and the Hydra of Lerna
(Hercule et l'Hydre de Lerne)

Water color over lead pencil
9⅞ x 8¼ in. (25.0 x 21.0 cm.)
Squared in lead pencil
Signed at lower right in pen and ink: *Gustave Moreau*
Inscription below at center in pen and ink: *l'Hydre*

Musée Gustave Moreau, Paris

One of the most important ensemble sketches for Gustave Moreau's large painting, which was shown in the Salon of 1876 and at the Universal Exposition of 1878 and was later bought by the collector Louis Mante of Marseilles. It is now in a private collection. In a careful effort to draw the monster accurately, Moreau made many studies of serpents, constantly copying illustrations in books which he consulted in the library of the Jardin des Plantes. As for the mountain setting, it can well be compared to rocky background planes in the paintings of Leonardo da Vinci which Moreau so greatly admired.   G.M.

L'Hydre ‑ Gustave Moreau

Gustave MOREAU

74 Salome

Pen and brown ink, heightened with gouache, on tracing
paper
11⅜ x 5¾ in. (29.0 x 14.5 cm.)
Signed at lower left: *Gustave Moreau*
Inscription at lower right: Salomé

Musée Gustave Moreau, Paris

There are many known variations of this theme which
was so essential in Moreau's work. The two most important are the painting first shown in the 1876 Salon,
now in the Huntington Hartford collection in New
York, and the water color entitled *The Apparition,* also
exhibited in the 1876 Salon and now in the Louvre with
the rest of the Hayem collection. This precise, detailed
study done on tracing paper reveals the accumulation
of a whole repertory of motifs which Moreau borrowed
from other sources—sometimes tracing them directly off
documents.

G.M.

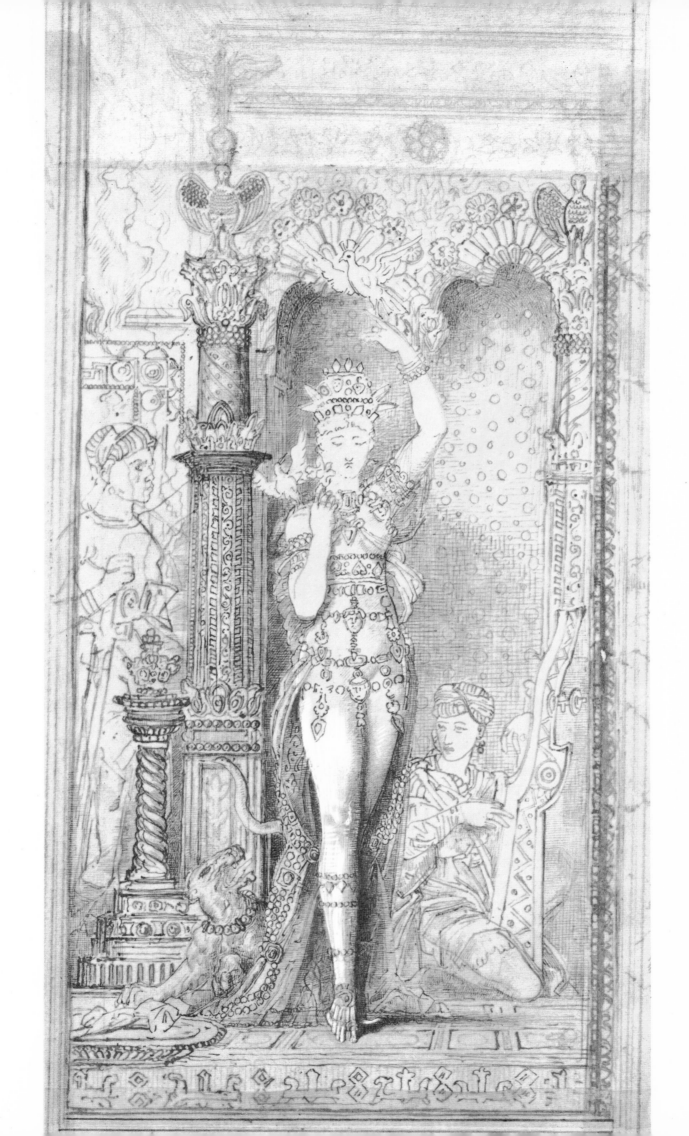

Gustave MOREAU

75 The City Mouse
and the Country Mouse
(Le rat de ville et le rat des champs)

Water color, pen and black ink, heightened with white
gouache, on tracing paper
11¼ x 8½ in. (28.5 x 21.5 cm.)

Musée Gustave Moreau, Paris

This sketch is one of the most beautiful of Moreau's
numerous studies for a group of sixty-three drawings
illustrating the *Fables de La Fontaine*, commissioned in
1879 by his friend Antony Roux. They were exhibited
in 1886 in Paris in the Galerie Goupil in Rue Chaptal.
The setting here is particularly sumptuous, done with an
elaborate network of pen lines enlivened by occasional
spots of bright color. It had been suggested to the artist
by Roux: "...choosing the Louis XIII style, which
would permit you to place on the table Benvenuto Cel-
lini ornaments, precious stones and gold..."

G.M.

Jean-Baptiste Camille COROT Paris 1796 - 1875

Corot studied with Michallon and Bertin in Paris, but his first extended stay in Italy from 1825 to 1828 was the most determining factor in his formative years. At that time he painted his sketch of the *Bridge of Narni,* subsequently exhibiting the finished painting in the 1827 Salon. With even his very first painted sketches, which were solidly constructed and luminous in quality, Corot took his place as the great landscapist of the nineteenth century. Upon his return to Paris he made many studies from nature and travelled all over France in search of sites before which he could place his easel; in fact he was one of the first artists to paint from life, and his numerous drawings bear witness to his incessant study and research. From 1831 on, but particularly after 1835, Corot regularly exhibited at the Salon. In his second and third voyages to Italy (1834 and 1843) he developed his own scientific investigations of light and of composition: (*View of Florence, View of Volterra, Tivoli, The Gardens of Villa d'Este*). New elements appeared in his landscapes which suddenly became peopled with nymphs and classical shepherds (*Homer and the Shepherds*). Around 1857 Corot began to make figures which were not much appreciated by the public, and in 1868 he painted *The Woman with the Pearl (La Femme à la Perle*). His last works, particularly his large charcoal drawings, reveal that as he grew older his inspiration became more and more lyrical and his vision more and more poetic.

G.M.

76 Young Woman Seated with her Arms Crossed (circa 1840)
(Jeune femme assise, les bras croisés)

Lead pencil on grey paper
8⅜ x 7½ in. (21.2 x 19.1 cm.)

Louvre - No. RF 3353

The simplicity of this person caught in such a natural pose, the sobriety of her dress, the gentleness of the chalk line which with great suppleness delineates her contours and delicately models the shadows and lights, all make this drawing one of the most beautiful examples of Corot's portrait work. Robaut places it between 1835 and 1845, and it is certainly comparable to contemporary drawings by Ingres and Delacroix.

G.M.

Jean-Baptiste Camille COROT

77 The Mill in the Dunes (1871)

(Le moulin dans la dune)

Charcoal, estompe, touches of brush and wash, heightened with white and red chalk, on gray-blue paper
8⅞ x 12⅜ in. (22.7 x 31.4 cm.)
Signed at lower left in charcoal: *Corot*

Louvre - No. RF 3707

There is a marked similarity between this drawing and the landscapes of Corot's latest period, which was characterized by his use of charcoal handled in large rapid strokes on colored paper, and by dramatic atmospheric effects. The drawing could without doubt have been executed, as Robaut maintains, during May-June 1871 in the outskirts of Douai, where the artist took refuge at the time of the Commune upheavals. In this same year he painted the *Belfry of Douai* which is now also in the Louvre.

G.M.

Jean-Baptiste Camille COROT

78　Young Girl in a Beret (circa 1831)
(Fillette au béret)

Lead pencil
11⅜ x 8¾ in. (29.0 x 22.2 cm.)
Signed at lower left in lead pencil: *Corot*

Musée des Beaux-Arts, Lille

Alfred Robaut, Corot's historian who catalogued all
his works in four volumes published in 1905, dates this
portrait circa 1831. The little girl is probably Corot's
niece, Louise-Laure Sennegon, who in 1833 became
Madame Baudot. Her painted portrait, signed and
dated 1837, is now in the Musée de la Ville in Semur.
Corot must have given this drawing, which can be considered one of his most important, to his friend the
painter Théodore d'Aligny, for in 1878 it was bought
by the town of Lille from the estate of his widow, Madame Aligny.

G.M.

Jean-Baptiste Camille COROT

79 The Apse of a Church in Caen
(circa 1830)
(L'Abside d'une église à Caen)

Lead pencil on cream-colored paper
11¼ x 9 in. (28.4 x 22.9 cm.)
Inscription at upper right in pencil: *Caen*
On the verso, in lead pencil, a young woman lifting her
arm up in the air, standing in profile facing right

Louvre - No. RF 8849

The motif which Corot was studying in this drawing
is, as we see from the note in the artist's handwriting, a
detail of a church in Caen, very probably the apse of
the church of Saint-Pierre. The fine and precise execution, achieved by means of a very sharp lead pencil, is
characteristic of Corot's early style as a draughtsman.
We find it again, for example, in the celebrated drawing
in the Louvre of a similar subject: *The West Façade of
Chartres Cathedral* (No. RF 23335). The subsequent
painting, also now in the Louvre, was finished in 1830.

G.M.

Charles-François DAUBIGNY Paris 1817 - 1878

At the age of seventeen Daubigny left for Rome and devoted a year to visiting the great museums of Italy. Upon his return he spent some time as restorer of the paintings in the Louvre, and then entered the studio of Paul Delaroche. In 1838 he exhibited his *View of the Church of Notre Dame de Paris* at the Salon, and, continuing to devote himself primarily to his vocation as a landscape painter, he rapidly acquired a wide reputation. Following his predilection for rivers, streams and ponds, he finally realized his personal dream: to lead a wanderer's existence on board a boat—"Le Botin"—guided only by the whims of his imagination and the attraction he felt for certain places, as Claude Monet was to do later. Daubigny belonged to the Barbizon School; above all he heralded the future studies of the Impressionists through his concern for capturing the fleeting elements of light and of the moment.

G.M.

80 Landscape with a Pond

(Paysage à l'étang)

Black chalk and pastel on gray paper
12¾ x 19¼ in. (32.5 x 49.0 cm.)
Signed at lower left: Daubigny

Boymans van Beuningen Museum, Rotterdam

The originality of this great drawing lies in its curious arrangement on the page, the water in the front plane suggesting that the artist had gone out into the middle of the pond to work "on the spot." The drawing is altogether typical of the work of the Barbizon group which Daubigny joined soon after 1840, and according to Carlos van Hasselt it could be dated circa 1860.

G.M.

Henri-Joseph HARPIGNIES Valenciennes 1819 - Saint-Privé (Yonne) 1916

Here again we have a pure landscapist whose history is inseparable from the Barbizon School. Harpignies came however from the north, having been born in 1819 in Valenciennes. His long life (he died at almost the age of one hundred in Saint-Privé in the Yonne district) was a gentle and personal hymn to Nature. He was first employed as a travelling salesman but he soon turned his voyages to better advantage and brought back from Italy, among other things, a *View of Capri* which was his debut exhibit in the 1853 Salon. Although his *Wild Ducks* (*Canards Sauvages*) was refused by the jury in 1863, he had other official compensations, being invited to London by the "New Water Colour Society" in recognition of his predilection for that medium. He excelled in woodland scenes. The delicate nuances of his work permitted him to capture the subtle poetry of forest undergrowth. No one was better able than he to seize the fugitive quality of a passing hour or the changing atmosphere of seasons. No one else could bathe the new leaves of spring in such magical waves of moonlight.

L.D.

81 Forest Undergrowth in Morvan

(Sous-bois dans le Morvan)

Water color
12 x 8⅝ in. (30.4 x 22.0 cm.)
Signed and dated at lower left: *H. Harpignies 1868*
Inscription at lower right: *Morvan*

Musée Fabre, Montpellier, No. 06.5.17

The rigorous execution and pictorial structure of this water color dated 1868, mark it as having been done in the period of the artist's greatest maturity.

Henri-Joseph HARPIGNIES

82   **A Lady Walking in a Forest**
(Promeneuse dans un bois)

Water color
6⅜ x 5⅛ in. (16.3 x 13.0 cm.)
Signed and inscribed at lower left: *H. Harpignies. Au
Docteur Paulet, bon souvenir, Mars 1869*

Musée Fabre, Montpellier, No. 06.5.18

This water color, like the preceding one, is part of the
group of twelve water colors by Harpignies which were
left to the Montpellier museum in 1906 by Doctor Vin-
cent Paulet, a retired Army official.

                                        G.M.

Théodore ROUSSEAU Paris 1812 - Barbizon 1867

When Rousseau's painting *Cows Coming down out of the Jura Mountains* (*la Descente des vaches dans le Jura*) was refused by the 1835 Salon, he took it upon himself to become an independent painter, working from then on outside of Paris, far from any official activity. He actually settled at Barbizon, in the Forest of Fontainebleau, where he was soon joined by other artists such as Dupré, Millet, Daumier, thereby forming the Barbizon School, of which he was the Master. Though Rousseau was essentially a landscape painter he can be called a realist by virtue of his direct observation of nature, which he stripped of all mythological accessories and even of all human presence. But he was most importantly a poet: a contemplative melancholy, thoroughly romantic spectator of the wildness of nature.

G.M.

83 Broom on a Moor

(La lande aux gênets)

Charcoal brush and brown wash, green pastel, heightened with white, on beige paper
23⅜ x 35 in. (59.5 x 89.0 cm.)

Musée Fabre, Montpellier, No. 876-3-140

This large drawing which, according to Jean Claparède was executed in the forest of Fontainbleau near Milly, is very pictorial in technique and is certainly representative of the profound influence exerted on Rousseau by the touching landscapes of seventeenth century Dutch painters. "... The entire soul of Rousseau, as I know it, is present in this simple germinal chalk sketch for some extremely good painting. Perhaps the quality would have been lacking had he ever finished it," wrote Théophile Silvestre to Alfred Bruyas on January 22, 1872. The dramatic atmosphere of a deserted moor is accentuated here by an effect of violent light piercing the clouds of the vast turbulent sky.

G.M.

Gustave COURBET Ornans (Doubs) 1819 - La Tour de Peilz (Switzerland)1877

Courbet, who was the son of a peasant family in Franche-Comté, came to Paris at an early age to enter the studio of Steuben. His real development came, however, through his own study of paintings by the great masters in the Louvre. Courbet's vast paintings such as *The Stone Breakers* (*les Casseurs de pierre*) and *The Burial at Ornans* (1850) caused a great deal of scandal because of their direct and realistic choice of subjects, and in 1855 his large canvas *The Studio*, which synthesized the philosophies and social aspirations of a whole generation, became a veritable manifesto of the Realist movement: "M. Courbet is a powerful worker and a savage and powerful will," wrote Baudelaire at the time. An artist "engagé", "involved in life," he was a friend of Proud'hon, the socialist, and took part in the political demonstrations of the Commune. When the column in the Place Vendôme was knocked down, he was compromised and was obliged in 1873 to flee to Switzerland, where he eventually died.

While Courbet is first and foremost a painter, he shows the same stylistic qualities as a draughtsman: realism in his choice of subjects, a predilection for portraits and landscapes, conciseness in his vision, and vigor in his execution.

G.M.

84 Portrait of Francois Sabatier

Black chalk
13⅝ x 10½ in. (34.5 x 26.8 cm.)
The signature *G.C.* seems to have been added later

Musée Fabre, Montpellier, No. 892.4.13

According to Jean Claparède, Courbet must have done this drawing in 1854, at the time of his visit with François Sabatier, a poet, linguist and amateur painter who owned property at la Tour de Farges, near Lunel. Among the archives of the Montpellier museum there is a manuscript note from François Sabatier leaving his collection to the museum in 1892, and enumerating among other items: "5th. My chalk portrait by Courbet" ("5° mon portrait au crayon par Courbet".) Such a drawing is typical of the direct vision and energetic style of Courbet as a portraitist.

G.M.

Jean-François MILLET Gruchy (Cotentin) 1814 - Barbizon 1875

Millet was the son of a peasant family in Cotentin and began his apprenticeship in Cherbourg with the painter Bon Dumoncel, in 1833. Thanks to a grant from the town of Cherbourg in 1837, he was finally able to study in Paris and there entered the studio of Paul Delaroche. His first works were portraits and genre scenes which he did in an eighteenth century manner but his personality as a Realist was established in 1848 when he exhibited *The Winnower (le Vanneur)* at the Salon. In June, 1849 he settled in Barbizon and began to take an interest in the life of the country people and their work: *The Sower (le Semeur)* shown at the 1850 Salon, Metropolitan Museum, New York, *The Gleaners (les Glaneuses)* from the Salon of 1857, Louvre. *The Angelus* was painted in 1859. His debut as a celebrity came at The Universal Exposition of 1867 where he exhibited nine paintings. His last works, such as *Spring,* Louvre, are closely related to the studies and research which the Impressionists were to pursue.

In his realistic choice of subjects Millet was able to create a new balance between nature and man, achieving a perfect integration of human beings into their natural settings. He was essentially a draughtsman who expressed himself soberly and grandly both in the black chalk studies which were to influence Pissaro and Van Gogh, and in his pastels and water colors which reveal a profound sensitivity marked by gravity and emotion.

G.M.

85 Self-Portrait

(Portrait de l'Artiste par lui-même)

Charcoal on grey-blue paper
22⅛ x 17½ in. (56.2 x 44.6 cm.)
Signed at lower right in charcoal: *J.F. Millet*

Louvre - No. RF 4232

According to Alfred Sensier and Paul Mantz this portrait represents Millet in 1847 at the age of thirty-three. It was at this time, in his modest lodgings in Rue Rochechouart in Paris, that Millet received his first visit from Sensier who was to become his great friend and one of the most fervent collectors of his work.

J. F. Millet

Jean-François MILLET

86 **Peasant Woman**
Carrying a Jug of Water
(La porteuse d'eau)

Pen and brown ink, brown wash, water color, over lead pencil
10½ x 13½ in. (26.7 x 34.5 cm.)
Signed at lower right in pen and ink: *J.F. Millet*

Louvre - No. RF 4659

Conceived as a painted sketch, this very accomplished water color dates from 1857-58, at the time when the theme of peasant women on the banks of a stream often appeared in the artist's pastels, paintings and drawings. The harmonious integration of human figures in a landscape is one of Millet's important stylistic achievements.

G.M.

Jean-François MILLET

87 The Cow Gate in the Snow

(La Porte aux vaches, par temps de neige) (1853)

Black chalk, estompe on beige paper
11⅛ x 8⅞ in. (28.2 x 22.5 cm.)
Signed at lower right with initials in black chalk:
J.F.M.

Louvre - No. RF 4159

This astonishing snow-scene has been identified as a
view of the outskirts of the Barbizon forest, and dated
as 1853 thanks to a letter which the artist wrote in
February 21, 1853, to Sensier: "I have made three quick
sketches of snow, one of which is called *Porte aux
vaches.* Perhaps I will do others." A painting of the
same subject, but with no people in it, is in the Wilstach
collection in Philadelphia. This motif reappeared in a
pastel which is now in the Boston Museum of Fine Arts.
We make note of the extremely sober retrait of Millet's
technique in such a study as this one: the snow is simply
evoked by the untouched white of the paper itself.

G.M.

Jean-François MILLET

88 **Page of studies**
(Feuille d'études)

Black chalk on gray-blue paper
10⅞ x 14¾ in. (27.6 x 37.5 cm.)

Louvre - No. RF 11.235

In the upper left-hand section is one variation on the
artist's recurrent theme: *The Shepherdess Leading her
Flock* (*La bergère ramenant son troupeau*). At the lower
left, one of the studies for *The Peasant Woman Feeding
her Child* (*Paysanne donnant à manger à son enfant*) or
The Porridge (*La Bouillie*) of which there exist many
others—particularly the ones in the Louvre, and a
heightened drawing in the Montpellier museum (cf. the
following plates). The painting itself of this subject,
which was exhibited in the 1861 Salon, is now in the
Marseilles museum.

G.M.

Jean-François MILLET

89 **Peasant Woman Feeding her Child**
(Paysanne donnant à manger à son enfant)

Black chalk
6¾ x 5⅜ in. (17.2 x 13.6 cm.)
Signed at lower right with initials in pen and ink: *J.F.M.*

Louvre — No. RF 11252

Among all the studies relating to *La Bouillie* we make special note of those in the Louvre (Nos. 10321 on the back, 10353, 10651, RF 5665, RF 5680). This one is very close, though reversed as a composition, to the study now in the Montpellier museum and reproduced here as Plate 90.

G.M.

Jean-François MILLET

90 The Porridge

(La Bouillie)

Black chalk, heightened with chalk
14⅜ x 11¾ in. (36.5 x 29.9 cm.)
Signed at lower right in black chalk: *J.F. Millet*

Musée Fabre, Montpellier — No. 876.3.121

One of Millet's numerous interiors lit by a single feeble
source of light (here the fire) which provided him with
pretexts for subtle studies in values and atmosphere.

G.M.

Jean-François MILLET

91 The Well Shed at Gruchy

(La maison du Puits à Gruchy)

Black chalk, heightened with white and pastel
14¾ x 18¼ in. (37.5 x 46.3 cm.)
Signed at lower right in black chalk: *J.F. Millet*

Musée Fabre, Montpellier — No. 876.3.124

According to M. Faré and H. Baderou this drawing shows the small buildings surrounding the house where Millet was born, in the village of Gruchy in the Gréville (Manche) Commune. It could be dated as 1854, for Millet did visit Gréville from June to September of that year after the death of his mother. The same motif is found again in a drawing, also highlighted, now in the Boston Museum of Fine Arts.

G.M.

Honoré DAUMIER Marseilles 1808 - Valmondois (Oise) 1879

Baudelaire was not mistaken when in 1845 he placed the work of Honoré Daumier on the same plane as that of Ingres and Delacroix. And we who know today what a great artist he was acknowledging, cannot forget that the celebrated caricaturist of *Charivari* and the *Medical Nemesis* (*Némésis médicale*) died poor, almost blind, and totally unknown at Valmondois in the Oise in 1879, at the age of seventy-one. Born in Marseille in 1808, Daumier was brought to Paris by his parents in 1815. There, little by little through his employment first as an usher at the Palais de Justice and then as a bookseller, he grew to know intimately the comings and goings of the courtroom and the streets which he was later to depict so vividly in *Men of Justice* (*Gens de Justice*), *Bon Bourgeois*, and *The Happiest Days of Life* (*Beaux Jours de la Vie*). Alexandre Lenoir, who was his teacher, gave him a taste for Rubens and for sculpture without suspecting that this pupil would someday be modelling a famous series of hallucinatory busts in "clay of fire" (the expression is Elie Faure's—"argile enflamée"). Daumier's ardent republican convictions placed him in the ranks of the opposition and inspired him from 1830 on to execute ferocious portraits which realistically portrayed the men of his time and immortalized their features and poses, without being in the least diminished in quality by the impulse of political satire which motivated the artist.

Daumier was first and foremost a draughtsman. His output was considerable (four thousand lithographs, many water colors, many woodcuts), and his extraordinary visual memory allied with the variety of media which he had at his command gave him the vibrant reality, the grandeur, to be called "master of the pathos of human forms in action" and to be considered a precursor of Rodin.
L.D.

92 The Amateur

(L'Amateur)

Water color and gouache over black chalk
17¼ x 14 in. (43.8 x 35.5 cm.)
Signed at lower left in brush and black wash over black chalk: *h. Daumier*

The Metropolitan Museum of Art, New York
Bequest of Mrs. H.O. Havemeyer, 1929. The H.O. Havemeyer Collection.

This important, highly-colored drawing, which is so pictorial in its execution, is one of the most celebrated versions of Daumier's recurrent theme of Amateurs (see particularly Plate 97). J. Adhémar dates it as 1865. The force of the artist's style is evident here in his simple balanced placement of the composition on the page. It depicts so truly the pose of a person seated comfortably in his armchair so as best to contemplate his collection. A dedication to Cléophus (the actor Alfred Baron) inscribed on a very similar drawing in the Boymans Museum in Rotterdam may be a clue to the identity of the present subject.
G.M.

Honoré DAUMIER

93 The Third-Class Carriage

(Wagon de troisième classe)

Water color, pen and black ink, over lead pencil
9 x 13 in. (23.0 x 33.0 cm.)
Signed below toward the center: *h. Daumier*

Collection O. Reinhart, Winterthur

This theme which Daumier so often used in drawing
and in lithography was a pretext for him to depict
people in repose. They are waiting for their journey to
end and have fallen into the poses most instinctive to
them—the ones which most differentiate them from
one another. In the first row a man is dreaming, a child
is sleeping, an old man is leaning on his cane and
thinking; in the second, a couple looks out of the
window, a woman sleeps with her head lowered, a
man sleeps with his head thrown back. The sureness of
the gestures accentuates the vitality which is so characteristic of Daumier's figures.

G.M.

Honoré DAUMIER

94 **The Butcher**

(Le Boucher)

Water color and lead pencil
10⅝ x 7½ in. (27.0 x 19.0 cm.)
Signed at lower left: *h. Daumier*

Collection O. Reinhart, Winterthur

There is a water color depicting a similar subject, entitled *The Pork-Butcher* (*Le Charcutier*), in which one finds the same authoritative execution and the same simplification of composition. It is in the Gerstenberg collection (see Venturi No. 101).

G.M.

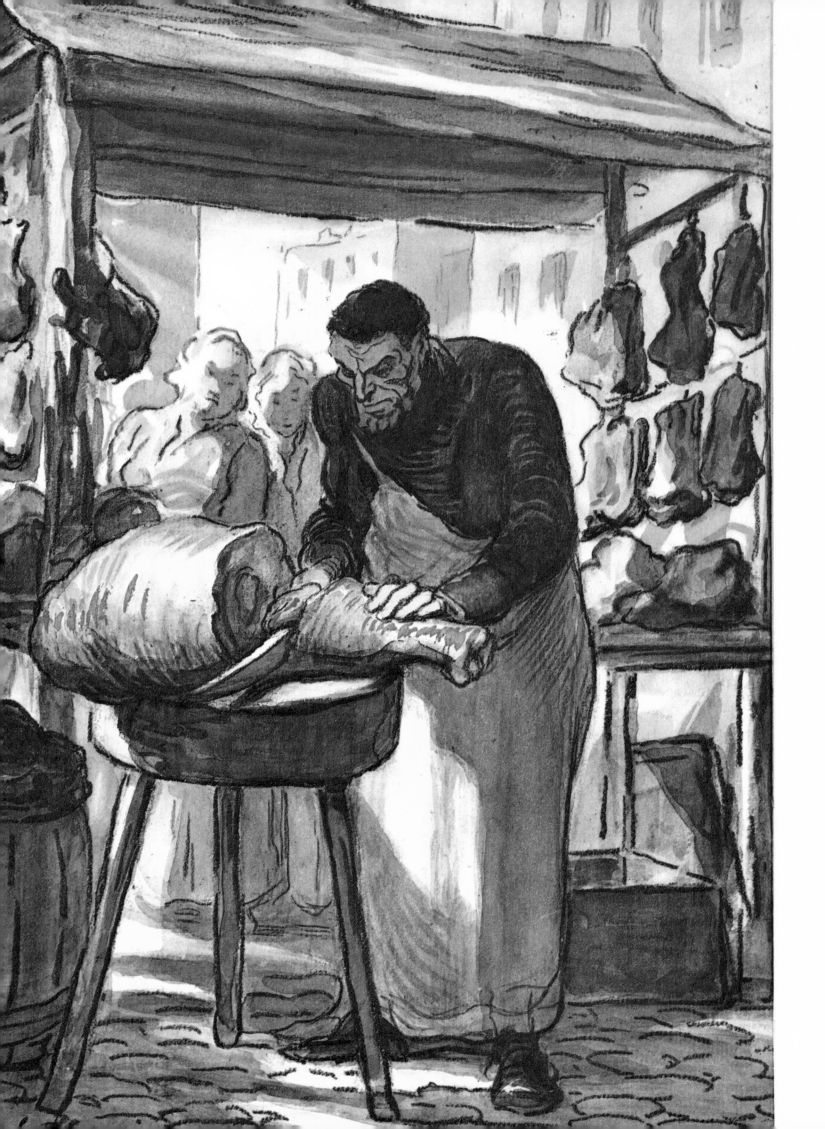

Honoré DAUMIER

95 The Intermission

(L'Entr'acte)

9⅝ x 13 in. (24.5 x 33.0 cm.)
Signed at lower right in pen and ink: *h. Daumier*

Collection O. Reinhart, Winterthur

This water color dated by J. Adhémar circa 1858 is
close to the painting on wood entitled *Orchestra Seats*
(*Les fauteuils d'orchestre*) now in the Chester Dale collection in New York. All the artist's interest here is
bent on a profound study of the numerous masculine
faces and on evoking the noisy agitation of this crowd
of people. As in most of Daumier's work, the subject is seen very close to.

G.M.

Honoré DAUMIER

96 The Politics of the Beer Drinkers

(La politique des buveurs de bière)

Pen and black ink, blue wash, over lead pencil
14½ x 11 in. (37.0 x 28.0 cm.)
Signed at lower left: *h.D.*

Collection O. Reinhart, Winterthur

The restraint of technical media and execution in this
drawing reveals the breadth of Daumier's vision. Even
in the most everyday scenes he is never merely anecdotal.

G.M.

Honoré DAUMIER

97   The Print Collectors

(Les amateurs d'estampes)

Pen and black ink, water color
7¼ x 9½ in. (18.5 x 24.0 cm.)
Signed at lower left in pen and ink: *h. Daumier*

Collection O. Reinhart, Winterthur

On a theme analogous to Plate 92, this drawing depicts two people in a room whose walls are covered with paintings. It is perhaps closest of all to the celebrated water color in the Louvre: *Three Print Collectors* (No. RF 4036) and to the one in the Victoria and Albert Museum in London: *Two Print Collectors*. Here Daumier has caught the spontaneity of the two men's different gestures: one is leaning forward, resting on his elbows, attentively examining an engraving, while the other has interrupted his scrutiny to throw a glance at the print in the foreground. The lateral lighting, so typical of Daumier's scenes gives strong relief to these figures.

G.M.

Honoré DAUMIER

98 **The Waiting Room**
(Salle d'attente)

Pen and black ink, wash, lead pencil
10⅜ x 8¼ in. (26.5 x 21.0 cm.)
Signed at lower right: *h.D.*

Collection O. Reinhart, Winterthur

This subject is related to the series of drawings and
lithographs of the *Third Class Carriage* (Plate 93)—a
theme which recurs as a leitmotiv in the work of
Daumier, changing according to his inexhaustible variety in trying different settings and compositions.

G.M.

Honoré DAUMIER

99 The Lawyer before the Tribunal

(L'Avocat devant le tribunal)

Black chalk pen and black ink, wash, over lead pencil
8⅛ x 11 in. (20.5 x 28.0 cm.)
Signed at lower left: *h.D.*

Collection O. Reinhart, Winterthur

The satirical verve and schematic execution of such a
piece heralds the celebrated series by Georges Rouault
of the same subject.

                                                G.M.

Honoré DAUMIER

100   The Lawyers
(Les Avocats)

Water color and lead pencil
5⅞ x 9¼ in. (15.0 x 23.5 cm.)
Signed at upper left: *h. Daumier*

Collection O. Reinhart, Winterthur

All the artist's attention is concentrated here, as it was
in *The Intermission* (Plate 95) on the masculine faces
whose strongly marked features are so clearly diffe-
rentiated.

G.M.

Honoré DAUMIER

101　A Peremptory Argument
(Un argument péremptoire)

Water color, pen and black ink, over lead pencil
7½ x 11 in. (19.0 x 28.0 cm.)
Signed and inscribed at lower left: *h.D. a mon ami Vial*

Collection O. Reinhart, Winterthur

Dé a mon ami Vial

Honoré DAUMIER

102 **The Two Doctors and Death**

(Les deux médecins et la mort)

Water color and lead pencil
12¾ x 11 in. (32.5 x 28.0 cm.)
Signed at lower left: *h. Daumier*

Collection O. Reinhart, Winterthur

Even more violently than in the preceding drawings,
Daumier is imposing himself here as a moralist, de-
nouncing the ignorance and blindness of two doctors who
can indulge in vehement discussion while Death is
actually carrying off the body of their patient.

This book has been printed and bound by
Amilcare Pizzi S.p.A., Milan, Italy.
Design by Abplanalp.

PHOTOGRAPHIC CREDITS:
Giraudon, plates 17, 48, 50;
Ektachrome Gerondal, plates 11, 78;
Musée Boymans, Rotterdam, plates 46, 80;
The Metropolitan Museum of Art, New York, plate 92.
All other plates, Jean-Edgar de Trentinian.

1767